Teach Yourself VISUALLY™

Car Care & Maintenance

Visual®

by Dan Ramsey and Judy Ramsey

WILEY

Wiley Publishing, Inc.

Teach Yourself VISUALLY® Car Care & Maintenance

Copyright © 2009 by Dan Ramsey and Judy Ramsey. All rights reserved.

Published by Wiley Publishing, Inc., Hoboken, New Jersey

No part of this publication may be reproduced, stored in a retrieval system or transmitted in any form or by any means, electronic, mechanical, photocopying, recording, scanning or otherwise, except as permitted under Sections 107 or 108 of the 1976 United States Copyright Act, without either the prior written permission of the Publisher, or authorization through payment of the appropriate per-copy fee to the Copyright Clearance Center, 222 Rosewood Drive, Danvers, MA 01923, (978) 750-8400, fax (978) 646-8600, or on the web at www.copyright.com. Requests to the Publisher for permission should be addressed to the Permissions Department, John Wiley & Sons, Inc., 111 River Street, Hoboken, NJ 07030, (201) 748-6011, fax (201) 748-6008, or online at http://www.wiley.com/go/permissions.

Wiley, the Wiley Publishing logo, Teach Yourself VISUALLY, and related trademarks are trademarks or registered trademarks of John Wiley & Sons, Inc. and/or its affiliates. All other trademarks are the property of their respective owners. Wiley Publishing, Inc. is not associated with any product or vendor mentioned in this book.

The publisher and the author make no representations or warranties with respect to the accuracy or completeness of the contents of this work and specifically disclaim all warranties, including without limitation warranties of fitness for a particular purpose. No warranty may be created or extended by sales or promotional materials. The advice and strategies contained herein may not be suitable for every situation. This work is sold with the understanding that the publisher is not engaged in rendering legal, accounting, or other professional services. If professional assistance is required, the services of a competent professional person should be sought. Neither the publisher nor the author shall be liable for damages arising here from. The fact that an organization or Website is referred to in this work as a citation and/or a potential source of further information does not mean that the author or the publisher endorses the information the organization or Website may provide or recommendations it may make. Further, readers should be aware that Internet Websites listed in this work may have changed or disappeared between when this work was written and when it is read.

For general information on our other products and services or to obtain technical support please contact our Customer Care Department within the U.S. at (877) 762-2974, outside the U.S. at (317) 572-3993 or fax (317) 572-4002.

Wiley also publishes its books in a variety of electronic formats. Some content that appears in print may not be available in electronic books. For more information about Wiley products, please visit our web site at www.wiley.com.

Library of Congress Control Number: 2009920042

ISBN: 978-0-470-37727-7

Printed in China

10 9 8 7 6 5 4 3 2 1

Book production by Wiley Publishing, Inc. Composition Services

Praise for the Teach Yourself VISUALLY Series

I just had to let you and your company know how great I think your books are. I just purchased my third Visual book (my first two are dog-eared now!) and, once again, your product has surpassed my expectations. The expertise, thought, and effort that go into each book are obvious, and I sincerely appreciate your efforts. Keep up the wonderful work!

—Tracey Moore (Memphis, TN)

I have several books from the Visual series and have always found them to be valuable resources.

—Stephen P. Miller (Ballston Spa, NY)

Thank you for the wonderful books you produce. It wasn't until I was an adult that I discovered how I learn—visually. Although a few publishers out there claim to present the material visually, nothing compares to Visual books. I love the simple layout. Everything is easy to follow. And I understand the material! You really know the way I think and learn. Thanks so much!

—Stacey Han (Avondale, AZ)

Like a lot of other people, I understand things best when I see them visually. Your books really make learning easy and life more fun.

—John T. Frey (Cadillac, MI)

I am an avid fan of your Visual books. If I need to learn anything, I just buy one of your books and learn the topic in no time. Wonders! I have even trained my friends to give me Visual books as gifts.

—Illona Bergstrom (Aventura, FL)

I write to extend my thanks and appreciation for your books. They are clear, easy to follow, and straight to the point. Keep up the good work! I bought several of your books and they are just right! No regrets! I will always buy your books because they are the best.

—Seward Kollie (Dakar, Senegal)

Credits

Acquisitions Editor
Pam Mourouzis

Development Editor
Jennifer Connolly

Copy Editor
Marylouise Wiack

Editorial Manager
Christina Stambaugh

Publisher
Cindy Kitchel

Vice President and Executive Publisher
Kathy Nebenhaus

Interior Design
Kathie Rickard
Elizabeth Brooks

Interior Photography
Dan Ramsey

Chapter Opener Photography
©iStockphoto.com/Skip O'Donnell

About the Authors

Dan Ramsey is the author of numerous books and articles on automotive topics. As a teacher, Judy Ramsey knows how to explain complex topics in simple terms. They founded the Fix-It Club® (FixItClub.com) offering common repairs made easy. Together, they also have maintained and repaired numerous cars and trucks.

Acknowledgments

The authors first thank technical advisor Loren Luedemann, an ASE Master Mechanic and full-time automotive technician with three decades of experience. Loren guided the development and illustration of this book. He's a top mechanic and friend!

Thanks to our pit crew: Ron Kendrick, Art Martinez, and Cesar Vasquez of Ron's Automotive, Willits, Calif. Thanks also go to Cathy Bouthillier, Dave Bouthillier, Dennis Nonneman, Katie Jeane, Joseph Haggard, Robert Fosnot, Jennifer Hayes, and Rod Keller of Little Lake Auto Parts, Willits, Calif.; Steve Fowler of Mendocino College, Ukiah, Calif.; Bob Bender of Ukiah (California) High School; and Don Buchanan of Coast Hardware, Willits, Calif. Thanks also to Jon Fitzsimmons of American Honda Motor Company, Bill Krenn and Kristin Brocoff of CarMD.com, and to the staff of the Willits (Calif.) KOA. Editorially, thanks for the efforts of Cindy Kitchel, Pamela Mourouzis, Jennifer Connolly, and Marylouise Wiack at John Wiley & Sons.

Thanks especially to our 1999 Honda Accord for serving as our primary automotive model for photos in this book. We have maintained it through 160,000 miles of trouble-free driving. Also, thanks to "Harrison," our Ford F250 pickup for assistance.

Numerous automotive products and brands are illustrated in this book's photos. The authors and publisher have not been paid for placement, nor do they endorse any product illustrated or described.

Table of Contents

chapter 1 Cars 101

chapter 2 Parts and Tools

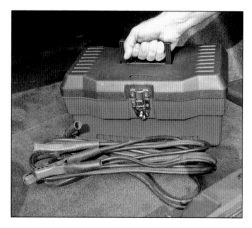

chapter 3 Preventive Maintenance

chapter 4 Cooling and Lubrication

chapter 5 Electrical

chapter 6 Fuel

chapter 7 Suspension and Steering

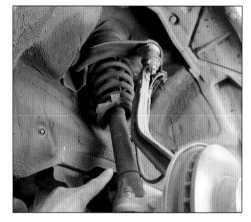

chapter 8 Brakes

chapter 9 Engine

chapter 10 Body

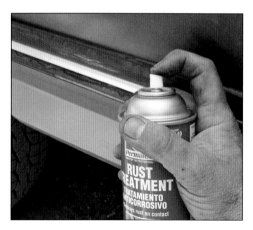

 **Easy Maintenance Guide**

Road Emergencies

chapter  1

Cars 101

Intimidated by your car? Afraid to peek under the hood and face the beast that carries you down life's highway? Don't be! Cars actually work on simple principles. If you know how they do their magic, you can control them better. And you can make them more fuel efficient. This first chapter gives you a good look under the hood, showing you how things work—and what to do when they don't. Starting now, you will never be frightened by your car—or your mechanic—again.

How Cars Work

Cars are seemingly complex, and becoming more so every day. However, they operate based on principles that everyone can understand.

Automobile History 101

An *automobile* is a self-propelled (auto) vehicle (mobile). The modern automobile design dates back 120 years to when gasoline-fueled engines were installed in carriages formerly pulled by horses. Soon, other components were added to make the ride smoother, faster, and more enjoyable for passengers. Within 25 years, more than 1 million cars and trucks were on the roads and the horse was nearly unemployed.

Primary Automobile Components

ENGINE

The *engine* in a car contains cylinders in which thousands of controlled explosions occur every minute the engine is running. The explosions occur when a mixture of gasoline and air is compressed and then ignited by an electric spark. The resulting explosions push the movable bottom wall of the cylinder down, which turns a shaft.

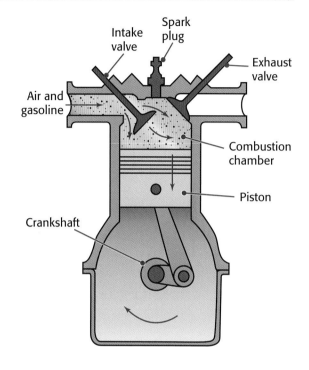

TRANSMISSION

A *transmission* transmits or moves the engine's rotation power to the wheels in stages using gears. Transmission gears function similarly to the gears on a ten-speed bicycle. A *manual transmission* requires the driver to manually select gears, while an *automatic transmission* selects gears automatically as designed.

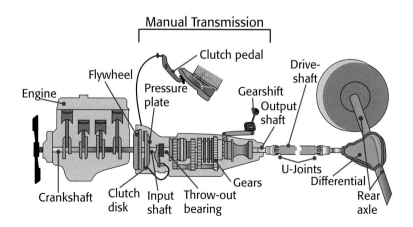

CONTINUED ON NEXT PAGE

SUPPORTING SYSTEMS

Everything else in your car supports either the engine and transmission or passenger comfort. To fulfill its function, your car needs:

- Cooling and lubrication (Chapter 4)
- Electricity (Chapter 5)
- Fuel (Chapter 6)

- Wheels and tires (Chapter 7)
- Brakes (Chapter 8)
- Body (Chapter 10)

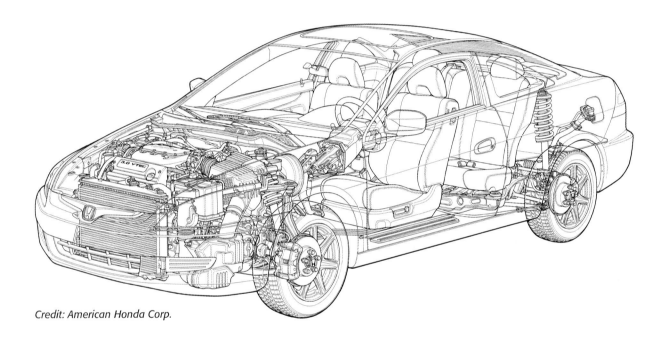

Credit: American Honda Corp.

TIP

Your Car's Book

For more specific information on your car, read the owner's manual that's probably in the glove compartment. Also, consider buying a repair manual from the manufacturer or an after-market publisher such as Chilton or Haynes, available at larger bookstores.

The best place to start getting to know your car is at the gas station. Take the time while the gas is pumping to distract yourself from the cost and spend some quality time with your car.

What can you do at the pumps? You can select the most appropriate fuel for your car, check fluid levels, do a visual inspection, and make sure that all systems are "go" before pulling back onto the highway.

Checking Out Your Car While Working the Pump

SELECT FUEL

Most fuel stations offer three grades of gasoline, and some also have one grade of diesel fuel. Gas energy is measured in *minimum* octane ratings—87, 89, and 91—marked clearly on the pumps. Which grade should your car use?

All gas-engine cars can operate using 87-octane gasoline, the least expensive grade. Some high-performance engines operate more efficiently with higher grade fuel. Your car's owner's manual will indicate which grade of gas the engine was designed to operate on. Alternately, use 87 octane unless the running engine has a pinging sound, called *knocking*, that may damage an engine. Then use higher octane fuel that doesn't knock.

Diesel is also a petroleum fuel, but not the same as gasoline. Don't use diesel in a gas engine or vice versa. Note that No. 2 diesel is pumped from a green nozzle.

CONTINUED ON NEXT PAGE

POP THE HOOD

For safety and security, the engine cover, called the *hood* (or *bonnet* in Britain), is latched into place. The hood release latch typically is located under the left side of the dashboard and is often marked HOOD.

1 Pull the hood lever inside the car.

2 Reach under the center of the partially opened hood and move the safety lever. (The car's owner's manual offers the specific location and instructions.)

3 Lift the hood and secure it in place. Many modern cars have a metal support bar across the front of the engine compartment. Lift the bar into place and insert the end into the designated hole on the bottom side of the hood.

4 Check the levels of engine oil and other liquids as described later in this book.

5 Perform a visual inspection for any obvious liquid leaks, rodent nests, loose caps, or other potential problems.

WALK AROUND

Once you've firmly closed the hood, walk around the car, inspecting the tires and underside for obvious problems or leaks. Inspect tires for wear, especially uneven wear, as described in Chapter 7 on suspension systems.

READ THE GAUGES

Your car has numerous lights and gauges that continually report the condition of its components. To read them, start the car or turn the ignition to the ACCESSORIES position.

- Ammeter gauge or light reports on how well the battery is being recharged by the alternator.
- Temperature gauge or light tells you if the engine is operating too hot.
- Fuel gauge indicates the level of fuel in the tank(s).

You will learn to read and interpret these gauges as well as the car's computer in coming chapters.

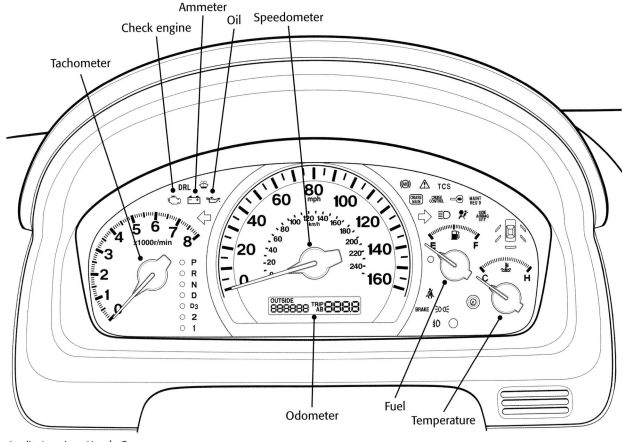

Credit: American Honda Corp.

Use Your Senses

In addition to looking at your car, pay attention to smells under the hood. The smells of burned rubber or plastic or of leaking fuel are warning signs that can alert you to potential problems. Also, listen to your car when it's running well so that you'll recognize the sound when it doesn't run well.

The Secret of Auto Repair

The complexity of cars over the past century, such as computer-controlled electrical systems, makes taking things apart and repairing them more difficult.

Fortunately, you don't have to rebuild a component anymore. It's easier—and often cheaper—to simply *replace the part*. In fact, that's what auto mechanics usually do. They replace rather than repair defective parts, and so can you, which is the *secret* of modern auto repair.

Knowing Your Car's Needs

PREVENTIVE MAINTENANCE

An important step in owning a trouble-free car—and minimizing costly work—is preventive maintenance. Replace oil, filters, and tires before they wear out and cause further damage. This book shows you how to perform basic preventive maintenance on your car step by step. Automotive maintenance is easy—when you know how.

OBSERVE

Modern cars are easier to drive; however, drivers today also have more distractions, such as cell phones, GPS, and the radio. Beginning at the gas station and continuing every mile that you drive, pay close attention to your car. As you learn more about how it works in this book, you'll detect more of the telltale signs that indicate what is expected and what is a potential problem.

REPLACE

Replacing a defective part can be a relatively simple job, depending on how difficult it is to get to the problem part. Many automotive parts can be replaced by any car owner. Others require additional instruction from this book or a specific-model repair manual. Still others are most efficiently replaced by a trained mechanic who has the tools and knowledge to make a difficult job look easy. This book helps you identify what you can replace and what you can't.

TROUBLESHOOT

Troubleshooting is simply comparing what you see to what you expect to see, and then using your knowledge to identify the cause. For example, you observe that the engine doesn't start as easily on mornings after it hasn't been driven for a few days. Knowing how cars work, you believe that a slow leak in a fuel line is robbing the engine of needed fuel when it starts up. A quick inspection confirms your observation and you have solved the problem—and saved yourself some money and future problems.

TIP

Troubleshooting Charts

A troubleshooting chart can save you hours of work and many dollars in replacement parts by helping you identify the source of an automotive problem. Your car's repair manual includes troubleshooting tips specific to the make, model, design, and components of your car. If the chart indicates more than one option, perform the easiest or least expensive before trying the others.

STEERING SYSTEM PROBLEMS

CONDITION	POSSIBLE CAUSE	RESOLUTION
Power steering pump leaks.	1. Fluid, cap and dipstick.	1. Check for indications of false leakage — overfilled reservoir, improperly installed, damaged or lost cap or dipstick.
	2. Loose or damaged hose connections.	2. Repair or replace as required.
	3. Leakage between reservoir and housing.	3. Repair or replace as required.
	4. Leakage at pump shaft seal area.	4. Replace shaft seal or pump.
Noise in steering column. (Squeak or creak)	1. Steering column cover interference.	1. Adjust or reposition as required.
	2. Steering column out of alignment.	2. Align or adjust as required.
	3. Lack of lubrication where horn brush contacts rub plate of steering wheel.	3. Lube or adjust as required.
	4. Loose steering column mounting bolts.	4. Tighten to specification.
(Clunk)	5. Flex coupling bottoming.	5. Align or adjust as required.
	6. Loose pot coupling to steering column bolt.	6. Tighten to specification.
	7. Improper steering gear mesh load.	7. Readjust to specification.
Excessive Steering Effort	1. Improper oversized tires.	1. Install correct tire and wheel combination.
	2. Tires not uniform.	2. Install correct tire and wheel combination.
	3. Tire pressure.	3. Adjust air pressure in tires.
	4. Misaligned flexible coupling (if so equipped) to gear interference.	4. Align or adjust as required.
	5. Steering wheel to column interference.	5. Align or adjust as required.
	6. Steering column alignment	6. Align or adjust as required (E-150 — E-350).
	7. Steering linkage or front axle spindle pins for a binding condition or lack of lubrication.	7. Lube, inspect, adjust o replace as required.
	8. Bind in front axle spindle thrust bearings.	8. Lube, inspect, adjust or replace as required.
	9. Steering gear adjustment.	9. Adjust to specification.

Do-It-Yourself or Not?

Intimidated by the complexity of taking care of your car? Don't be. Owners have been successfully maintaining and repairing their cars for decades. In a couple of pages, you'll learn how trouble-shooting and making repairs is even easier than it was two decades ago. You just need knowledge and the proper tools.

KNOWLEDGE

The primary difference between you and a $90+-an-hour auto mechanic is knowledge. The mechanic has gone to school to learn about how cars run, diagnostics, and parts replacement. You can pick up the knowledge needed for basic car care and maintenance from this book. With experience, you may decide to tackle increasingly complex repairs on your car. Car care isn't an all-or-nothing task. You can do the jobs that you are comfortable with and leave the heavy lifting to your well-chosen mechanic.

TOOLS

Another clear difference between mechanics and the typical car owner is tools. A mechanic or repair shop has thousands of dollars invested in specialized tools and diagnostic equipment, while the owner may have a $50 toolbox. Fortunately, you often can rent more expensive tools for difficult jobs.

The bottom line is that you have options. You can take better care of your car—and be ready to handle problems—by learning more about your car and performing increasingly difficult jobs.

Where is a qualified and honest mechanic when you need one? Well, the best time to find one is when you *don't* need one and when your car doesn't have an emergency that needs to be taken care of.

Knowing When You've Found "The One"

Start looking for a fair and competent mechanic as you take on more responsibility for the care of your car. As you learn more about how your car operates and how to diagnose problems, you'll also learn more about mechanics. The more you know about how your car works, the easier it will be to recognize a trustworthy mechanic. You'll discover that most are specialized: One who may be specially trained in automatic transmissions probably doesn't know as much about fuel injection systems.

The National Institute for Automotive Service Excellence (ASE) and other trade groups offer courses and certification tests for automotive technicians and parts clerks. An ASE mechanic who is certified in all car systems earns the Master Mechanic designation. Of course, if you need only a qualified transmission mechanic, you can select one with ASE certification in transmissions rather than one who does all repairs. Also, some repair shops earn AAA approval.

TIP

Compare Shop Rates

Many auto mechanics estimate the time required to complete a repair by using recommendations in a flat rate manual. They multiply the time estimate by their hourly shop rate to determine the labor rate. The higher the shop rate, the more expensive the labor charge will be.

Car Computer Basics

Wouldn't it be great if you could read the mind of your car's computer, just like your mechanic does with engine-analysis tools? You can!

OBD-II

WHAT IS OBD-II?

All new cars, light trucks, SUVs, and minivans sold in North America since 1996 are required to have a connection for on-board diagnostics (OBD). The second version, OBD-II, has been the standard for more than a decade. Europe has had EOBD for new gasoline cars since 2001 and diesel cars since 2004.

OBD-readers plug into a connection on the vehicle, read the computer data, and report parameter identification numbers (PIDs). These PIDs can be decoded. P1456, for example, indicates that an EVAP system leak is detected in the fuel tank area. In plain English, the gas cap is loose. Mechanics have been using on-board diagnostics readers for many years.

FINDING OBD-II DIAGNOSTICS TOOLS

The good news for consumers is that handheld OBD-II diagnostics tools are now available for less than $100! One popular version is the CarMD (www.carmd.com). With the included instructions and software, car owners can read and interpret the car's diagnostics system. You can use these handy tools to:

- Quickly diagnose problems during an emergency.
- Discuss an automotive problem more accurately with your mechanic.
- Verify the findings of your mechanic.
- Check your car for problems before taking it in for a state-required smog test.
- Check cars and light trucks you are considering for purchase.

USING THE OBD-II

There are four simple steps to using a consumer-level OBD-II diagnostics tool:

1 Insert the data link connector (DLC) into the car's receptacle. (Check your car owner's manual for the DLC location.)

2 Within 10 seconds, turn the ignition key to the ON (*not* START) position.

3 Wait for the data download to complete.

4 Refer to the tool's printed documentation, computer software, or website to decode the data.

Chapter 5 offers more detailed steps for using a consumer OBD-II diagnostics tool. Also refer to instructions that come with the unit.

FAQ

How can I know for sure if my car's computer can be read by OBD-II analyzers?

All 1996 and newer vehicles are required to be OBD-II (also known as *OBD2*) compliant. In addition, some 1994 and 1995 cars can be read by OBD-II analyzers. To verify, open your car's hood and look for the VEHICLE EMISSION CONTROL INFORMATION label located on the underside of the hood or near the radiator. If it is compliant, the label will say "OBD-II Certified." Some light-duty diesel pickup trucks and recreational vehicles (RVs) also are OBD-II certified.

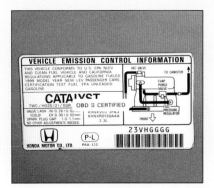

2

Parts and Tools

A car is simply a collection of parts designed to work together toward moving you down the road. To function properly, these parts need to avoid their two enemies: heat and friction. If they don't, they must be replaced. For this, you'll need tools. This chapter helps you identify and choose the parts and tools you may need to care for and maintain your car.

Model Identification

With more than 1 billion cars manufactured over the past century, a system is needed to identify the make and model of each vehicle. It's especially important when you need to buy a part. Here's how to easily identify your car.

Vehicle Identification Numbers

HOW THE VIN OPERATES

Vehicle Identification Numbers (VINs) are unique 17-digit numbers that identify individual cars and trucks manufactured since 1980. Before that, each manufacturer had its own coding system. Standardizing VINs has made auto manufacturing, parts selection, and repair easier. They are used in a variety of ways to identify specific vehicles and their components. VINs are used by:

- State motor vehicle departments
- State and local police
- Insurance companies
- New and used car dealers
- Auto repair shops
- Fleet owners

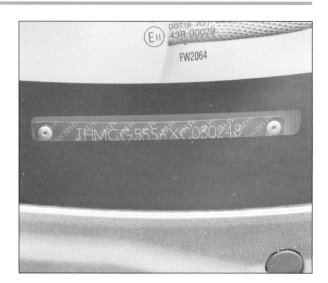

FIND THE VIN

You can find your car's VIN in one or more of these locations:

- On the dashboard at the driver's-side corner of the window.
- On the driver's-side door or doorpost, when opened.
- On the firewall, the wall separating the engine compartment from the passenger compartment.

You'll also find it on your car's state registration and probably your auto insurance card.

DECIPHER THE VIN

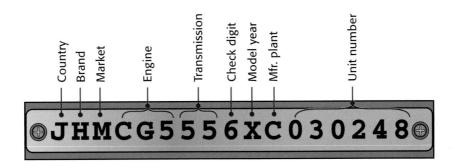

Buying major car parts often requires that you have the car's VIN to ensure that you get the correct replacement part from the auto parts supplier. You don't need to be able to decipher your VIN to buy parts, but it's fun and easy to do. As you read through the following list to find out what the specific digits represent, you can also see examples for each by checking out the accompanying photos on the previous page, which show the VIN JHMCG5556XC030248. The key to your car's VIN is located in the manufacturer's service manual or online at the manufacturer's website.

- **Digits 1–3:** The World Manufacturer Identifier indicates the manufacturer's name and in what country the vehicle was built.

  JHM: Honda (H) manufactured in Japan (J) for the U.S. market (M)

- **Digits 4–8:** The Vehicle Descriptor identifies the model, body style, and engine.

  CG555: Accord with VTEC engine (CG5); four-door sedan with manual transmission (55)

- **Digit 9:** Digit 9 serves as the Check Digit; it is used to ensure that the VIN is valid.

  6: the check digit

- **Digits 10–17:** The Vehicle Identifier can be either digits the manufacturer uses to identify specific options or a sequential serial number.

  XC030248: 1999 model year (X); built in the Sayama, Saitama (C) plant as unit number 30,248

VIN decoders are available on the Internet and at some auto parts stores.

Note: In addition, some manufacturers put a part number sticker on every body component. This number can help you find a replacement part. If it's missing, it may mean that someone already has replaced the part, such as after an accident.

TIP

Buying a used car? Not sure if it has been in an accident or stolen and salvaged? Want to know what primary service has been done on the car? You can use its VIN to find out. For a fee, services such as CarFax.com and AutoCheck.com offer reports on modern VINs, including title, odometer, problems (major accidents, salvage, theft, fire), and registration (police car, taxi, lease, fleet car).

Parts Identification

Some parts and accessories you buy for your car fit the make and model of your car only. Others fit other cars made by the same manufacturer. Still others are universal and fit thousands of car models made by dozens of manufacturers. So you need to be able to identify and describe the part you need.

Steps to Identifying Any Part of Your Car

Following are four basic questions that can help you identify any part on your car. After answering these questions, you only need to be armed with the VIN and you can easily get the part that your car needs.

1. WHAT IS IT?

This book is designed to help you visually identify the various systems and parts on your car. You'll soon be able to recognize an alternator, brake pad, fuel filter, radiator hose, and other replaceable parts. In addition, you'll know how to select the most appropriate oil, transmission fluid, and coolant for your car.

2. DOES IT HAVE A PART NUMBER?

All modern cars are built with interchangeable parts. An air filter for your car will fit thousands, maybe millions, of other cars; it doesn't have to be custom-built to your vehicle. These interchangeable parts typically are identified by numbers or other codes to make replacing them easier. For example, you can purchase a new strut using the part number on the old unit.

Be aware that aftermarket (not the original) parts manufacturers may use different numbers, but your parts supplier will have thick books on the parts counter that cross-reference original-equipment manufacturer (OEM) part numbers with those from the manufacturers the store carries.

3. WHAT DOES IT INCLUDE?

When replacing a part on your car, you need to determine what is and isn't included. For example, if you're buying a replacement alternator, does the new one include the bolts needed to install it—or should you use the old bolts or buy new ones separately? Fortunately, your auto parts supplier can help you answer this question. If in doubt, save yourself a trip to the parts store by calling and asking them what is included.

4. DO YOU NEED NEW OR REBUILT PARTS?

You have choices when it comes to auto parts: You can purchase new, used, or rebuilt parts; the decision often comes down to economics.

Buying new parts makes sense if the parts are small and less expensive, but the difference in price between larger new parts and their rebuilt counterparts may be 50 percent or more. If you need an alternator or an engine, the difference can be from a few hundred to a few thousand dollars.

TIP

Larger parts that you replace can be rebuilt and resold by the auto parts industry. Therefore, the auto parts store may charge you more if you don't bring in the bad part you're replacing. To make sure that you do, they may require that you pay a core charge, refundable when you bring in the old part.

Buying Auto Parts

There seems to be an auto parts store on every corner in many towns. In addition, discount stores and hardware stores sell popular auto parts. But there are a few things you can do to find the best places to buy the parts you need.

After you find reputable places to purchase parts, take the part you want to replace with you, if possible. Of course, make sure that you have the vehicle's VIN and any part numbers that you've found.

Where to Buy Your Parts

As you learn more about your car, visit auto parts suppliers in your area. Browse, learn more about what's available, and compare prices. As you begin making purchases, identify local parts sources with the most knowledgeable clerks.

TIP

Use an auto log or a small notebook to start a record of the maintenance that you perform on your car. In addition, record the part numbers of the components that you buy most frequently: oil, oil filter, air filter, and so on. You can also record prices paid for these parts to determine the best place to buy them in the future.

Oil is your engine's blood. Without it, your car's engine would soon die. But don't worry: Selecting the right oil for your car is relatively easy.

Choose the Right Oil

Engine oil is identified by *viscosity* (thickness) and service ratings:

- Viscosity is rated using standards developed by the Society of Automotive Engineers (SAE). Most modern engine oils have two viscosity ratings: cold and hot. For example, many cars use oil of 10W-30 viscosity: 10 (thinner) when the engine is cold (on startup) and 30 when the engine is hot (running).

- Service ratings for oil are developed by the International Lubrication Standardization and Approval Committee and are referred to as API ratings. Whatever oil you buy for your car should meet or exceed the minimum required by the engine manufacturer. The oil container's label specifies the API rating (an example is SJ) as well as its viscosity.

Synthetic oils are okay to use if they meet the API and viscosity ratings required by the engine manufacturer. However, they are more expensive. In most cases, the best oil for your car is the one recommended by the manufacturer. The owner's manual includes the specifics.

Your Car's Toolbox

The right tool can make the difference between a 15-minute part replacement and a day of frustration. However, you can spend thousands of dollars on automotive tools—as your mechanic does—and still not have the right tool for every job. Fortunately, you can do most auto maintenance and many repair jobs with just a few basic tools and a little know-how.

Gather the Tools You Need

WRENCHES

Wrenches turn nuts and bolts.

- **Closed-end wrenches (1)** give you more grip.
- **Open-end wrenches (2)** are easier to use in tight places.
- **Socket wrenches (3)** are easier to use than hand wrenches.
- **Adjustable wrenches** allow you to adapt the wrench to the nut or bolt you're turning.

Wrenches are sized in inches (standard) and metric. Most modern cars use metric measurements. You may also need special Allen or Torx wrenches for some jobs.

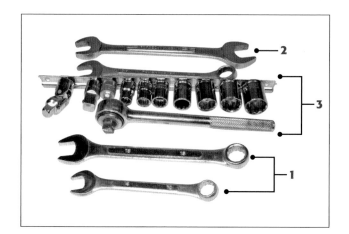

SCREWDRIVERS

Screwdrivers turn screws. To select the appropriate screwdriver, match the screwdriver to the screw head style and size. Various tip designs are used on cars, but slotted **(1)** (commonly called flathead) and cross **(2)** (commonly referred to as Phillips-head) are the most popular. As you tackle more advanced car maintenance jobs, consider buying an assortment of screwdriver tips **(3)** for your toolbox.

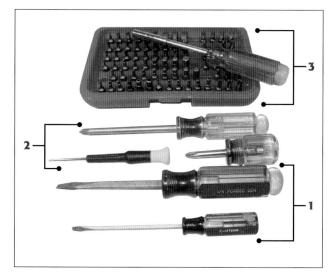

PLIERS

Pliers grab, twist, or hold parts. Some types include:

- **Groove-joint pliers (1)** are adjustable to fit many jobs. They are often referred to by the brand name, Channellock.
- **Slip-joint (2)** pliers have two different width openings.
- **Long-nose (3)** (also called needle-nose) pliers have pointed tips.
- **Flat-nose (4)** pliers have squared-off, flat tips.
- **Pincer pliers (5)** are good for removing nails.

Locking pliers can hold a part while it is being turned. Some pliers also serve as wire cutters.

ELECTRICAL TESTER

Modern car electrical systems are powered by 12 volts of electricity stored in the automotive battery. Testing electrical components requires a tool called an electrical tester, volt-ohmmeter (VOM), or multimeter. They're all the same thing. Instructions with the tester will demonstrate how it is used to test electrical systems and components. This book also includes basic electrical tests you can easily perform on your car (see Chapter 5).

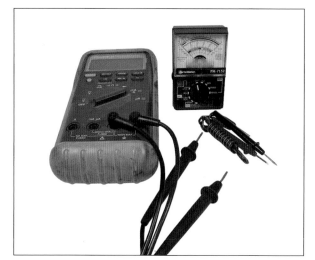

FAQ

Why do most auto repair tools use the metric system?

Because automobile manufacturing is an international industry, most modern cars are built using the metric system. Auto parts, such as nuts and bolts, are measured in millimeters (mm). Tires also use the metric system in sizing. An inch is 25.4mm. Your toolbox should have metric wrenches from 8 to 19mm for general work. Don't try to use standard tools on a metric part or vice versa; you might damage the part.

CONTINUED ON NEXT PAGE

HANDY TOOLS

In addition to wrenches, screwdrivers, and pliers, there are other basic tools that are helpful. They include:

- Tire pressure gauge (for checking air pressure in tires)
- Shop rags (for cleaning up)
- Funnel (for pouring fluids)
- Oil receptacle (for collecting drained oil)

ADVANCED TOOLS

As your car knowledge grows, you may tackle bigger jobs, such as jacking the car up and using a creeper (shown at right) to access the underside. You'll also want stands to safely support the car's weight. Other advanced tools include an engine hoist and specialized auto body tools. Your toolbox will grow with your experience.

DIAGNOSTIC TOOL

If you plan to do more than just maintain your car, consider purchasing an electronic diagnostic tool as described in Chapter 1 (one example is CarMD). With it, you can read problem codes reported by your car's computer system and often diagnose problems at the side of the road. Consumer OBD-II units cost less than $100, and basic units can be purchased for less than $50. Make sure the unit you select includes a printed or electronic decoder so you can decipher the codes.

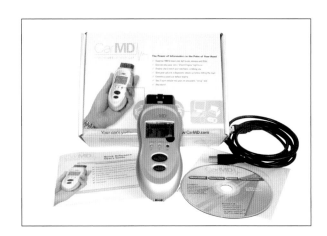

TOOLBOX

Once you've selected your basic car care tools, you can begin searching for an appropriate toolbox to house them. For most car owners, a heavy-duty portable plastic toolbox with trays for common tools and spare parts is the best solution. However, you can start with a heavy-duty bag or even an old purse. Your toolbox should be sturdy, but not too heavy to lift when full. If you're building an automotive care area in your garage, you can purchase a larger toolbox on rollers. However, you still may want a smaller box with basic tools that you can keep in your vehicle for on-the-road emergencies.

WHERE TO KEEP YOUR TOOLBOX

Keep your toolbox where you need it. If you are changing oil and doing other preventive maintenance, your toolbox can stay in the garage or a nearby storage area. If you expect to have to do some emergency repairs, the toolbox should be in the trunk of your car. Many consumers have two toolboxes, one for preventive maintenance and another for emergency repairs.

TIP

Can't afford $500 or more to buy a special tool that you'll use only once? Consider renting it. Most large auto parts stores and equipment rental centers rent larger and more specialized auto care tools. Rates can be as much 10 percent of the cost of the tool for the weekend—a $500 tool rents for $50—but renting is much cheaper and more efficient than buying a one-time tool or taking your car to a mechanic.

Cars are heavy. Many of their parts are moving. Some parts are electrical. Others are hot. How can you *safely* work on your car? Common sense will guide you.

Safety Rules

Common-sense safety tips include the following:

- Don't allow any open flames near gasoline; it is a flammable liquid that will ignite with a spark.
- Make sure that the vehicle is in park, the parking brake is on, and the wheels are blocked so the car doesn't move when you're working on it.
- Do not work on parts that are hot. Allow the car or part to cool for at least 15 minutes before touching potentially hot parts.

- If you jack the car or a wheel off the ground, firmly place a support under the frame before working under it.

  Caution: When working on a car, always make sure that children or pets are not where they can get hurt.

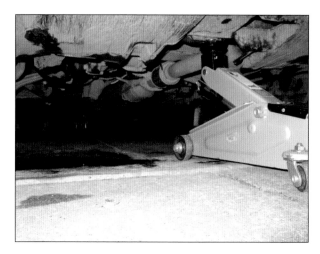

- Be cautious working around the battery, as it stores electricity and chemicals.

- Your car's computer is a sensitive—and expensive—component. Be careful and follow the manufacturer's instructions when connecting a diagnostic tool or working with electrical wiring.

- A running engine has whirling blades and belts and other moving parts that can catch clothes, skin, or tools, so be cautious. The more you know about how your car works, the safer you will be as you work on it.

TIP

Refer to Your Owner's Manual

Your car's owner's manual includes specific safety tips for working on your car. For example, it notes the designated location for jacking up the car, as well as how to use the manufacturer's jack safely.

3

Preventive Maintenance

Don't let that mass of metal and plastic in your driveway intimidate you. With a little bit of guidance from this chapter, you will easily be able to take control of your car's future and extend its functional life by many years and thousands of miles with preventive maintenance.

If you think that preventive maintenance involves performing task after task and reviewing checklist after checklist every day before getting into your car, you might be tempted to throw preventive maintenance out the window. However, after reading this chapter, you'll find out just how easy preventive maintenance really is. For instance, you'll discover that you follow the same pattern of preventive maintenance for all of your car's fluids: Check the fluid level and then add fluid if necessary.

By the time you reach the end of this chapter, you'll see that preventive maintenance tasks require mere minutes or even seconds of your time and need to be done only once or twice a month. Just a bit of your time can go a long way toward extending your car's life as well as helping to prevent costly repairs. In addition, you'll know what to do when something goes wrong. And perhaps most important, with the guidance from this chapter, you'll have such confidence in your abilities that you'll quickly earn bragging rights to say, "I work on my own car."

As Chapter 2 explains, oil is the engine's blood. How can you determine whether the engine has sufficient oil to operate? You can check it yourself.

Checking the level and condition of engine oil takes less than five minutes and should be done every time you fuel up, or at least once a month. All you need is a clean paper towel or rag.

Check the Oil Level

1 Make sure the engine is cold and the car is level before proceeding. You are measuring the oil level at the bottom of the engine.

2 Find the oil dipstick in the engine compartment. It typically is located near the center and often has a metal loop on the top.

3 Pull the oil dipstick all the way out of the tube.

4 Wipe the tip of the dipstick clean with a paper towel or rag.

5 Visually inspect the clean dipstick to identify the location of the FULL mark and the ADD mark.

6 Reinsert the dipstick until the handle is firmly seated in the oil tube.

7 Remove the dipstick, hold it horizontally, and read the level of the oil. If the level is at or below the ADD mark, add oil.

Add Oil

To add oil, follow these steps:

1. Select oil of the same viscosity and service rating (see page 23 in Chapter 2) as is in your engine. If in doubt, refer to the owner's manual.

2. Remove the oil filler cap mounted on top of the engine and set it aside. Most caps screw off.

3. Insert an oil funnel in the oil filler hole. Disposable paper funnels are available at auto parts stores.

4. Slowly and carefully pour oil into the funnel as needed to bring the oil level up to the FULL mark.

   Caution: DO NOT fill oil beyond the FULL line on the dipstick. Excess oil can cause internal problems in the engine.

5. Replace the oil cap and recheck the oil level.

FAQ

How can I tell if my oil is in good condition?
Visually inspect the oil. As a reference, look at the color and consistency of new oil. Used oil should be darker, but not black. In addition, oil that is milky contains water and indicates a deeper engine problem. Also rub the oil between your fingers to ensure that it is smooth and not gritty. If in doubt, change the oil and filter (see Chapter 4).

Automatic Transmission Fluid

Cars use either manual or automatic transmissions (AT) to transfer engine power to the wheels. Checking the level and condition of AT fluid can prevent problems in automatic transmissions. (See Chapter 4 for manual transmission care.)

You need a clean paper towel or rag, a long-neck funnel to add fluid, and just a few minutes once a month for newer cars and more frequently for older cars.

Check AT Fluid Level

Note: *Some newer cars have a sealed transmission. AT fluid in these vehicles should be checked and filled following the manufacturer's instructions.*

1. Make sure that the engine is warm and idling and the car is level before proceeding. You are measuring the fluid at the bottom of the transmission.

2. Place the transmission in PARK (P) or NEUTRAL (N), as recommended by the manufacturer, and set the parking brake.

3. Find the automatic transmission fluid (ATF) dipstick in the engine compartment. It typically is near the rear and often has a metal loop on the top.

4. Pull the dipstick all the way out of the tube.

5. Wipe the tip of the dipstick clean with a paper towel or rag. AT fluid is dyed red so it isn't confused with engine oil.

6. Visually inspect the clean dipstick to identify the locations of the FULL and ADD marks.

7. Reinsert the dipstick until the handle is firmly seated in the ATF tube.

8. Remove the dipstick, hold it horizontally, and read the level of the AT fluid. If the level is at or below the ADD line, add AT fluid.

Add AT Fluid

To add automatic transmission fluid, follow these steps:

1 Select AT fluid as recommended by the manufacturer. An auto parts clerk can help you select the appropriate AT fluid for your model car. If in doubt, refer to the owner's manual.

2 Insert a long-neck funnel in the ATF dipstick hole.

3 Slowly and carefully pour AT fluid into the funnel as needed to bring the fluid level up to the FULL mark.

Caution: DO NOT fill beyond the FULL line on the dipstick. Excess AT fluid can cause internal problems in the automatic transmission.

4 Replace the dipstick and recheck the fluid level.

FAQ

How can I tell if my AT fluid is in good condition?

AT fluid is a red hydraulic fluid. If it is light brown, it is nearing the end of its service life and should be replaced soon. If it is dark brown, it should be replaced immediately. If it's gray, it may have water in it and should be replaced immediately. Also feel the AT fluid. If it is gritty to the touch, replace it, as metal particles or other contaminants can quickly ruin an automatic transmission.

Brake Fluid

When you press the brake pedal, hydraulic brake fluid activates the brakes at each wheel. If brake fluid is low, the brakes can feel "soft" or weak.

Fortunately, checking brake fluid is easy and quick. With a see-through brake fluid reservoir, do a visual check every time you open the engine compartment. If your compartment is metal, you may need to remove the reservoir top to check the brake fluid level once a month. You only need a clean paper towel or rag.

Check the Brake Fluid Level

1. Find the brake fluid reservoir in the engine compartment. It typically is near the rear of the compartment and made of transparent plastic.

2. Visually determine whether the fluid is within operating range between FULL and ADD.

3. If necessary, add brake fluid as recommended by the car manufacturer.

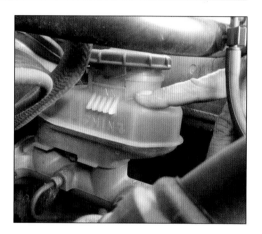

Add Brake Fluid

To add hydraulic brake fluid, follow these steps:

1. Select brake fluid as recommended by the manufacturer. An auto parts clerk can help you select the appropriate fluid for your model car. If in doubt, refer to the owner's manual. Most modern cars require brake fluid designated "DOT-3."

2. Carefully wipe the top of the reservoir with a clean paper towel or rag, and unscrew the cap.

3. Slowly and carefully pour brake fluid into the reservoir as needed to bring the fluid level up to the FULL mark.

   Caution: Don't fill brake fluid beyond the FULL line. Excess brake fluid can cause internal problems in the master brake cylinder. Also, don't allow brake fluid to touch the paint on your car.

TIP

Water is brake fluid's enemy. Moisture that gets into brake fluid can cause the aluminum and cast iron parts to deteriorate. It also can get into the anti-lock system and make it fail. Not good. When replacing brake fluid, be especially careful not to allow moisture into the reservoir.

When you turn the steering wheel, hydraulic fluid in the power steering unit makes steering your car much easier. But if the fluid level is low, your car will be more difficult to steer.

Checking the level of power steering fluid is easy and takes just a minute of your time while you're checking other fluid levels in the engine compartment. You may need a clean paper towel or rag.

Check the Power Steering Fluid Level

1 Make sure that the engine is warm, but NOT RUNNING, before proceeding.

2 Find the power steering pump in the engine compartment. It typically is near the front of the compartment and made of metal with a cap on the top. The pump is powered by an engine belt.

3 Carefully wipe the top of the pump and cap with a clean paper towel or rag and unscrew the cap.

4 Hold the dipstick horizontally and read the level of the fluid. If the level is at or below the ADD line, add power steering fluid.

CONTINUED ON NEXT PAGE

Add Power Steering Fluid

To add power steering fluid, follow these steps:

1 Select power steering fluid as recommended by the manufacturer. An auto parts clerk can help you select the appropriate fluid for your model car. Recommended fluids vary with the manufacturer. If in doubt, refer to the owner's manual.

2 Wipe the top of the pump and cap with a clean paper towel or rag, and then unscrew the cap.

3 Carefully pour power steering fluid into the reservoir as needed to bring the fluid level up to the FULL mark.

Caution: DO NOT fill fluid beyond the FULL line on the dipstick. Excess power steering fluid can cause internal problems in the power steering pump.

FAQ

Are all of the hydraulic fluids that a car uses interchangeable?
No!

Though the automatic transmission, brakes, and power steering systems all use hydraulic fluid, each fluid is different. Use only the type and grade of fluid recommended by the car manufacturer. Refer to the owner's manual for specifications. In addition, make sure that the fluid you use is not contaminated with water, dirt, or other elements that can damage internal parts. If in doubt, buy a new container of a reputable brand of fluid. Cheap or questionable hydraulic fluids are false economy.

Although windshield washer fluid is a convenience rather than a necessity of car operation, it can make driving easier and safer. So take an extra moment to check the washer fluid level.

All cars have a windshield washer reservoir; some use a dipstick, and others are made of clear plastic with ADD and FULL marks on the side, which makes it easy to visually check the fluid level.

Check the Washer Fluid Level

1 Find the windshield washer reservoir in the engine compartment. It typically is near the driver's side and made of transparent plastic; the cap may have an emblem depicting a windshield wiper.

2 If the fluid level is marked on the outside of the reservoir, visually check the level to make sure it is between FULL and ADD.

3 If it is not marked on the outside of the reservoir, wipe the top of the reservoir and cap with a clean paper towel or rag and lift the cap. Then hold the dipstick horizontally and read the level of the fluid. If the level is at or below the ADD line, add windshield washer fluid.

Add Washer Fluid

To add windshield washer fluid, follow these steps:

1 Select windshield washer fluid as recommended by the manufacturer. An auto parts clerk can help you select the appropriate fluid for your driving needs and climate. If in doubt, refer to the owner's manual.

2 Wipe the top of the reservoir and cap with a clean paper towel or rag, and then lift the cap.

3 If using prepared washer fluid, pour it into the reservoir to bring the fluid level up to the FULL mark. If using concentrated window washer fluid, prepare it as instructed on the packaging before pouring it into the reservoir.

TIP

Should you buy prepared or concentrated windshield washer fluid? Prepared washer fluid, sold in one-gallon plastic jugs, is convenient to use, but not always convenient to store. Concentrate takes more effort to mix and add, but is easier to store. In addition, concentrate can be sprayed or poured onto a windshield to clean stubborn road grime.

Belts

Your engine not only powers the wheels but also turns the radiator fan, alternator, power steering pump, and other devices using flexible belts called *drive belts*. As an easy but important part of semi-annual preventive maintenance, make a visual inspection of your drive belts.

Check Belt Condition

At the front of your car's engine, there are round pulley wheels. Each one has a drive belt wrapped around it and another pulley or two. You want to make sure your drive belts are in good condition because if they break, something important will stop turning.

You can visually inspect drive belts in the engine compartment, looking for belts that are:

- Cracked
- Oil-soaked
- Glazed
- Torn

Caution: *Never attempt to inspect a drive belt's condition or tension when the engine is running. The turning belts can pinch your fingers or grab loose hair, clothing, or jewelry.*

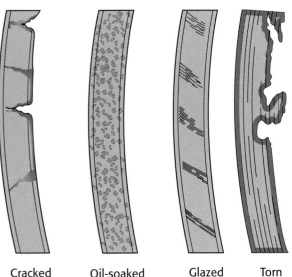

Cracked   Oil-soaked   Glazed   Torn

Check Belt Tension

Another problem that drive belts face is that they stretch with age. If the belt's tension is reduced, the pulley that's being driven (such as the alternator or power steering pump) will not work as efficiently.

The easiest way to check drive belt tension is to know what it should be. Mechanics have special tools for measuring belt tension. You can learn to check visually by asking a mechanic to show you how much tension each drive belt should have. Most belts can be compressed a specific amount midway between pulleys. Simply record or remember how much you can compress the belt with your finger or a tool, and periodically recheck the belts.

You also can visually inspect any adjusters, such as a support and bolt that holds the alternator in place and tensions the belt. Has the adjuster moved?

Note: *Some drive belts have automatic tensioners that adjust the belt as needed.*

FAQ

What should I do if a belt needs adjustment or replacement?

You can buy replacement belts at auto parts stores. Some belts are relatively easy and intuitive to install:

1. Loosen the tension adjuster.
2. Remove and replace the drive belt.
3. Replace the drive belt tensioner as recommended by the car's manufacturer.

Many people new to car care hire a mechanic to do the job—and watch and learn while it's done. Once you are comfortable with the process, the steps are included in Chapter 9. Make sure that the new belt is an *exact replacement* for the old one.

Battery

At the front corner of your car's engine compartment, you see the rectangular battery, your car's electrical power source. The battery powers the starter, computer, radio, and other important components. It is recharged by the alternator. Every time you open the hood, perform a quick visual inspection of your car's battery to help you identify problems that could leave you stranded.

Check the Condition of the Battery

Visually inspect the battery for the following potential problems:

- Obvious damage to the battery case
- Corrosion at the terminals or cables
- Loose cables on the terminals
- Liquid

Caution: *Be very careful about touching the battery, as it can burn you. In addition, any liquid on the surface could be water—or it could be caustic battery acid. Assume that it is acid. White dust on the terminals is corrosion.*

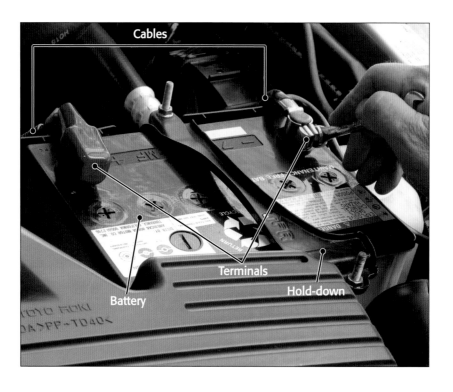

Clean the Battery

You can clean corrosion on your car's battery with a solution of baking soda and water to neutralize the acid. Alternately, you can use club soda or an unsweetened soda pop. You also need a brush, such as an old toothbrush, and a rag. For safety, wear protective eyewear, as the corrosion dust is acidic.

FAQ

What should I do if I think the battery is "dead"?

If the battery doesn't have enough power to start your car or power the headlights, do the following:

1. Check the battery connections to make sure they are clean and tight. If they are loose, tighten them and allow the engine's alternator to recharge the battery for at least 20 minutes before testing again.

2. Use a multimeter (see page 73 in Chapter 5) to test voltage between the positive (+) and negative (−) battery terminals. Voltage should be between 12 and 14 volts on the meter's DC scale.

3. Take the battery to a mechanic or auto parts store to recharge it.

4. If necessary, replace the battery with a new one of the same size and group (see pages 76–77 in Chapter 5).

Note: *Batteries are heavy. Be careful when attempting to move one.*

Coolant and the Radiator Cap

Coolant is the liquid in your car's radiator that circulates through the engine to keep it cool. Modern cars have a coolant reservoir tank that holds excess coolant for the radiator.

The radiator cap keeps the coolant from getting out. It takes just a minute to check the coolant level and radiator cap condition on your car.

What to Check

CHECK THE COOLANT LEVEL

To check the coolant level, follow these steps:

1. Find the coolant reservoir in the engine compartment. It typically is near the front of the compartment and made of plastic. It is connected to the radiator neck (below the cap) by a small hose.

2. Visually check if the fluid is within operating range between FULL and ADD. If necessary, add coolant.

CHECK THE RADIATOR CAP

The radiator cap is relatively easy to check. Look for obvious leaks around its perimeter. If you see coolant leaks around the radiator cap, first make sure the cap is tight. If it isn't, replace it.

TIP

Most car manufacturers recommend a coolant that is made up of 50 percent antifreeze and 50 percent water. Check your car's owner's manual for specifications.

REPLACE COOLANT

To add radiator coolant, follow these steps:

1 Select coolant as recommended by the manufacturer. An auto parts clerk can help you select the appropriate fluid for your car. If in doubt, refer to the owner's manual.

2 Wipe the top of the reservoir and cap with a clean paper towel or rag, and then lift or unscrew the cap. Some caps have a pressure release valve that must be lifted first.

3 Pour coolant into the reservoir as needed to bring the fluid level up to the FULL mark.

REPLACE THE RADIATOR CAP

To replace a radiator cap, follow these steps:

1 Select an exact replacement radiator cap at an auto parts supplier. The cap must be the same type, size, and pressure rating as designated by the car's manufacturer. Most caps are designed to release coolant if radiator pressure exceeds 13 to 16 pounds per square inch (psi).

2 Remove the old cap, clean the radiator neck opening if needed, replace the cap, and turn it until it locks in place.

Caution: DO NOT turn the radiator cap when the engine is hot. Because the system is pressurized, the coolant can be hotter than boiling water! When pressure is released, the coolant can spray out and burn your skin. Instead, wait until the radiator is cool to the touch before opening the cap.

 TIP

While you're checking the coolant and radiator cap, take a look at the radiator hoses that carry coolant to and from the engine. One hose is at the top of the radiator, and the other is at the bottom. Visually inspect their condition. See pages 54–55 in Chapter 4 for instructions on hose inspection and replacement.

Windshield Wipers

With the engine compartment hood closed, you can quickly inspect the condition of your car's windshield wipers. You may already suspect wiper problems. Driving in the rain may remind you that the wipers are sticking or not clearing the water from the windshield efficiently. You also should inspect windshield wipers monthly during drier months to make sure they are ready for a sudden storm.

Check the Wiper Blades

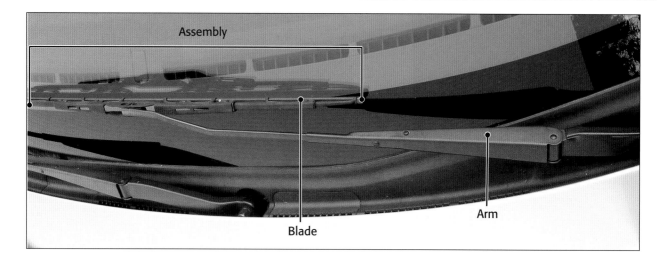

1. From one side of the windshield, grab the wiper assembly at the center and lift it away from the glass. Most wiper arms lock the spring assembly in position so that you don't have to hold it as you inspect components.

2. Assess the blade's condition. If it is torn or worn, replace the wiper blade.

3. Inspect the assembly. Make sure that the connection to the wiper arm is in good condition. As needed, reconnect or replace the wiper assembly.

4. Inspect the wiper arm. If it is damaged or the spring isn't holding the wiper assembly on the windshield with sufficient force, the wiper will not do a good job. As needed, repair or replace the wiper arm.

Note: *To test wiper blades, use the windshield wiper control to squirt wiper fluid on the windshield. Then watch to make sure that the blades work efficiently.*

Replace the Wipers

On some cars, you can replace the blade without replacing the assembly. On others, you need to purchase a complete assembly. Wiper arms are more difficult to replace; follow the manufacturer's instructions for installing and adjusting wiper arms.

To replace wiper blades or assemblies, follow these steps:

① Measure the length of the old wiper blade from tip to tip. If possible, remove the old blade and take it to an auto parts supplier for an exact match.

② Identify the type of connection that the blade has to the assembly or that the assembly has to the wiper arm. Blades typically slide into an assembly from one end, following a notched track. Assemblies connect to the arm using a clip or pin.

③ Install the wiper blade or assembly following the instructions in the package. In most cases, installing the unit is simply the reverse process of removing the old one.

④ Pour water on the windshield and turn on the wipers to test them. Be ready to turn off the wipers quickly if there is a problem.

TIP

Replace Wipers in Pairs

Even though only one wiper may have problems, replace both of them at the same time. They both will have equal wear, and the second unit will probably fail soon as well. Also, remember to write down the wiper model number in your car book for future reference.

Tires

Tires are containers of pressurized air. Early cars rolled on solid tires, and passengers suffered as a result. Modern tires are designed to last longer and be more trouble-free than tires of old. Even so, there are things you can do to keep tires in good shape. The most important is to make sure that the air pressure in each tire is sufficient to minimize damage and wear. Visually inspect tires for proper inflation once a week, and check pressure once a month.

Check Tire Pressure

To check tires for proper inflation, follow these steps:

Note: *Check tire inflation pressure when the tire is cold, not after a long drive. Heated air expands and gives you a different reading.*

1 Select a tire pressure gauge. Pencil-shaped gauges are adequate and easy to carry in a pocket. Round gauges are more accurate, easier to read, and more expensive. Gauges are also available with digital readouts.

2 If necessary, unscrew the cover on the tire's valve stem. You may need to remove a wheel cover with a pry tool for easier access.

3 Press the gauge firmly onto the tire's valve stem. The pressure inside the tire activates the gauge.

4 Read the inflation pressure, the highest number indicated on the gauge.

5 Compare the actual pressure with the recommended pressure. The correct tire pressure is listed in the vehicle owner's manual or on a decal stuck on the driver's side doorjamb. Don't use the pressure rating on the tire's wall, as it is a maximum rating.

After you've verified that all tires are at their proper inflation pressure, take a look at the tire profiles so that you can more easily recognize underinflation in future inspections.

Check Tire Condition

The physical condition of tires is also important to safety. Excess wear can indicate improper inflation, suspension system mis-alignment, or road damage. Visually inspect the condition of your car's tires at least once a week for optimum service.

To check tire condition, follow these steps:

1 Check tire treads. Modern tires have wear indicators molded into them. When the wear bar shows across the width of the tread, the tire is beyond the manufacturer's limits. States have tire tread minimums. Most state laws require that tires have at least $\frac{1}{16}$ inch of tread remaining.

2 Check for uneven wear. Visually inspect each tire for uneven wear caused by underinflated tires or incorrect wheel alignment. Chapter 7 includes instructions on rotating tires for more even wear, as well as replacing tires.

3 Check the sidewalls. The sides of tires can be damaged and cause blowouts. Visually check both sidewalls of the tire, the one you usually see and the one on the other side of the tire. You may need to lie down (on a clean spot) and use a flashlight to visually inspect the tire. Alternately, run your hand over both surfaces to find any cracks, bulges, or other sidewall damage.

FAQ

What about the spare tire?

Don't forget to check the condition of the car's spare tire. Most spare tires in passenger cars are stored under a panel in the trunk floor and are accessed from the trunk. Pickup trucks and some SUVs store the spare under the rear frame, and the spare is accessed from under the truck. Note that most spare tires are designed to be driven only a short distance and at reduced speeds.

4

Cooling and Lubrication

Engines run hot and fast. To keep them cool and running smoothly, engines have cooling and lubrication systems. Taking care of your car means managing these two systems. This chapter shows you how. The rewards include an engine that will serve you for many thousands of miles.

How the Cooling System Works

How hot is it? Metal inside your engine can run as high as 1,000°F (538°C). Your car's cooling system reduces the coolant's temperature by using air. It does so with a water pump, thermostat, radiator, hoses, and cooling fan. The car's heating system uses some of the excess heat.

Elements of the Cooling System

COOLANT

Coolant, a mixture of antifreeze and water, absorbs the engine heat. For most climates, the recommended mixture is 50/50. Antifreeze is made with either ethylene glycol (poisonous) or propylene glycol (safer). Other safe antifreeze products include phosphate-free ethylene glycol and organic antifreezes that contain no phosphates.

In addition to cooling an engine, ingredients in antifreeze minimize rusting of metal parts and lime deposits that can clog the system. Cooling systems should be periodically flushed of all coolant. (See "Replace the Coolant," on page 56.)

WATER PUMP

The coolant is circulated through the engine and radiator by a *water pump.* The pump draws hot coolant from chambers in the engine, called *jackets.* It then pumps the coolant through a hose to the radiator, which has a cooling fan.

THERMOSTAT

To keep the engine within the optimal temperature range, a *thermostat* is installed at the water pump. The thermostat regulates the flow of coolant through the upper radiator hose and into the radiator. Thermostats are designed to begin opening at about 195°F (105°C). The hotter the coolant gets, the more the thermostat opens to allow more coolant to circulate.

Cooling System

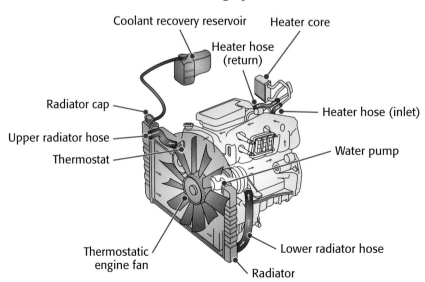

Coolant recovery reservoir · Heater core · Heater hose (return) · Radiator cap · Upper radiator hose · Thermostat · Heater hose (inlet) · Water pump · Thermostatic engine fan · Lower radiator hose · Radiator

HOSES

Coolant flows from the engine to the radiator and returns from the radiator to the engine through radiator hoses. In addition, the heater system has two smaller hoses that siphon off coolant and deliver it to the heater core. Hose clamps attach the hoses to the engine and radiator.

RADIATOR

The *radiator* is a heat exchanger. It transfers engine heat, captured by the coolant, to the air that passes through the radiator. The radiator is a series of tubes with thin fins that expose the heat (not the coolant) to the surrounding air. The coolant enters the top of the radiator, flows out the bottom, and returns to the engine through a hose.

COOLING FAN

A *cooling fan* is mounted on the engine side of the radiator to draw air over the radiator's finned tubes. The fan's rotation is powered by an electric motor or by the engine through a drive belt. For greater efficiency, the cooling fan typically is surrounded by a plastic shroud. When the car is moving very fast, the fan isn't required; some models' fans are slowed down or shut off with an automatic fan clutch.

HEATER CORE

The engine's heat can also be used to warm the car's interior. A *heater core,* similar to a small radiator, is mounted inside the passenger compartment, typically under the passenger side of the dashboard. Some heater cores are mounted in the engine compartment, and heat is ducted to the passenger compartment. Heat is controlled by the comfort thermostat.

Other components of your car's cooling system include temperature sensors or senders that report coolant temperature to your car's computer and gauges.

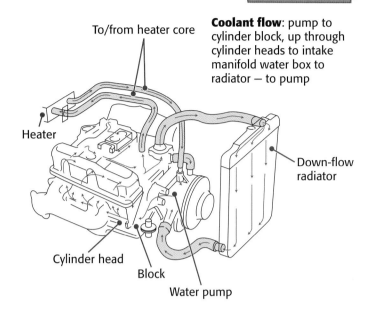

To/from heater core

Coolant flow: pump to cylinder block, up through cylinder heads to intake manifold water box to radiator — to pump

Heater

Down-flow radiator

Cylinder head

Block

Water pump

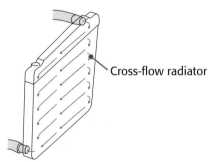

Cross-flow radiator

Replace the Hoses

An engine's cooling system is made of metal and rubber. Obviously, the rubber components, the hoses, will need more frequent replacement than metal parts.

Replacing the Hoses

Cooling system hoses are relatively easy to replace using basic tools. Following are instructions for inspecting and replacing cooling system hoses.

1. INSPECT THE HOSES

Whenever you open your car's hood, take a moment to check the condition of the radiator hoses. Because the insides of these hoses handle high temperatures, they break down before the outsides, so you may not know they're bad before they fail—unless you inspect them closely.

There are two or three cooling system hoses in the engine compartment: upper and lower radiator hoses and maybe a smaller bypass hose between the engine and the water pump. The upper hose typically fails first.

To inspect radiator hoses, follow these steps:

1 Make sure that the engine and radiator are not hot.

2 Visually inspect each hose for obvious breakdown:

- Cracks or leaks
- Swelling
- Excessive softness
- Excessive hardness

3 Squeeze each hose to estimate its firmness.

4 If in doubt about a hose's condition, replace it.

Note: For future reference, inspect the condition of new hoses so you know what they look and feel like, and compare them to those on your car.

TIP

Heater hoses can be inspected and installed similarly to radiator hoses.

2. INSTALL NEW HOSES

Replacement radiator hoses must be of the correct inside diameter, length, and shape. Mechanics recommend that you replace all radiator hoses at the same time. In addition, make sure that you purchase high-quality hoses so you don't have to install replacements for a while. Take your car's model data (refer to Chapter 2) to find the correct replacement parts. Here's how to install new hoses:

1 Make sure that the engine and radiator are cool to the touch.

2 Place a large drain pan under the radiator *drain cock* (the small plug at the bottom of the radiator) and carefully open the cock. Drain the coolant below the level to be worked on. If you are replacing both the upper and lower hoses, drain the entire coolant system. (See "Replace the Coolant" on the next page.)

3 Loosen and remove the old hose clamps. Spring clamps may require a special tool, available at auto parts stores.

4 Use a utility knife to carefully cut the ends of the old hose for easier removal.

5 Remove the hose from the radiator and engine.

6 Clean the hose connections at both the radiator and the engine.

7 Dip the new hose ends in coolant to lubricate them.

8 Slip *new* hose clamps over the ends of the new radiator hose.

9 Install the hose ends on the radiator and engine connections, overlapping by approximately 1 inch.

10 Place the hose clamps approximately ¼ inch in from the ends, and tighten them with pliers.

11 Add new coolant as needed.

Replace the Coolant

Car manufacturers recommend that you replace engine coolant every two years. You can also flush the system at the same time to remove built-up contaminants. When you replace the coolant, you may also want to replace radiator hoses to minimize the chance of a roadside emergency.

Replacing the Coolant

1. CHECK THE ANTIFREEZE

Once a year, typically in the fall, check your car's antifreeze level to make sure that it is adequate for the upcoming winter. You need a coolant hydrometer or test strips, available at auto parts stores. To check antifreeze, follow these steps:

① Make sure that the engine and radiator are cool to the touch.

② Open the coolant reservoir cap or the radiator pressure cap.

③ Insert the hydrometer hose in the coolant.

④ Squeeze the hydrometer bulb and slowly release to draw coolant into the test chamber.

⑤ Read the indicator to determine the freeze point of the coolant. Add coolant as needed.

Note: You can use antifreeze test strips following the manufacturer's instructions. See photo at right.

2. DRAIN THE COOLANT

To drain engine coolant (antifreeze and water), follow these steps:

① Make sure that the engine and radiator are cool to the touch.

② Place a large drain pan under the radiator drain cock and carefully open the cock. Drain the coolant into the container.

③ Carefully pour the old coolant into sealable containers for disposal.

Note: Some states consider ethylene glycol coolant hazardous waste. Contact the local waste management office to determine the safest method for disposal.

3. FLUSH THE COOLANT SYSTEM

Coolant flushing kits (shown at right) are available at most auto parts stores. The kits include specific instructions for use. In general, follow these steps:

1 Make sure that the engine and radiator are cool to the touch.

2 Find the heater core return line, typically at the rear of the engine compartment.

3 Place a drain pan beneath the hose to catch coolant.

4 Cut through the return line with a knife.

5 Install the flushing adapter and hose clamps.

6 Remove the radiator cap and attach the nozzle to the radiator neck as directed.

7 Place a drain pan beneath the nozzle to catch the coolant.

8 Attach a water hose to the return line adapter and turn it on, as recommended by the kit manufacturer. The water back flushes the system, forcing coolant out of the radiator nozzle.

9 Remove the nozzle and cap the flushing adapter. The adapter will remain in the system to make future coolant flushing easier.

10 Install new coolant.

4. INSTALL NEW COOLANT

1 Make sure that the engine and radiator are cool to the touch and that the drain cock at the bottom of the radiator is closed.

2 Check the owner's manual to determine the appropriate amount and mixture of antifreeze and water in the coolant.

3 Place a funnel in the radiator neck.

4 Carefully pour the recommended amount of coolant into the radiator through the funnel and neck.

5 Add water to the radiator as needed.

> **Note:** Alternately, you can mix the antifreeze and water in a container before pouring it into the radiator.

6 Install the radiator cap, preferably a new one.

7 Fill the coolant reservoir as recommended by the manufacturer.

8 Run the engine to remove trapped air and recheck the coolant level.

Inspect the Radiator and Heater

The radiator is the largest component of your car's cooling system. It requires size to disperse the heat from the coolant into the passing air. Proper care can keep it working longer.

The excess heat pulled from the engine doesn't go to waste. It is recycled. The hot coolant also is circulated through the heater core to warm air in the car's interior as directed by the heater controls.

Keeping the Radiator and Heater Working

INSPECT THE RADIATOR

The radiator is a large collection of finned tubes that enable passing air to cool the liquid inside. To inspect the condition of a radiator annually, follow these steps:

1. Make sure that the engine and radiator are cool to the touch.

2. Use a water hose with a nozzle to clean the radiator exterior and cooling tubes to make problems easier to see.

3. Visually inspect all parts of the radiator for possible leaks or damage. As coolant is green, leaks often are outlined in green. Alternately, leaks may be outlined in red caused by internal rust.

4. If leaks are found, replace the radiator or have it repaired.

INSPECT THE HEATER

A car's heater is a small radiator, except that the heat is used to warm the passenger compartment rather than be dispersed into the atmosphere. Symptoms of a bad heater core include frequent fog on the inside of the windshield and/or wet spots on the carpet under the core. To inspect the condition of the heater annually, follow these steps:

1. Make sure that the engine and heater are cool to the touch.

2. Find the heater core, typically either under the passenger side of the dashboard (shown at right) or at the rear of the engine compartment.

3. Visually inspect the heater core for possible leaks or damage. Look for green or red discoloration, as mentioned in the preceding section, "Inspect the Radiator."

4. If you find leaks, replace the heater core.

5. Check the condition of the heater hoses for condition and replace them as needed, following the instructions under "Install New Hoses" on page 55.

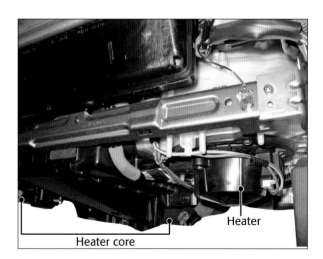

Heater

Heater core

Replace the Radiator

As noted in Chapter 1, the secret of auto repair is replacement rather than repair. To replace a radiator, follow these steps:

Note: Refer to the car manufacturer's service manual or aftermarket repair manual for instructions specific to your make and model.

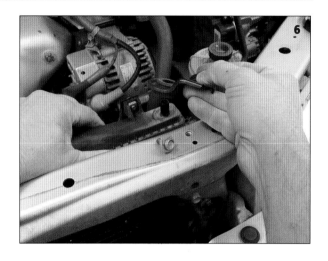

1 Make sure that the engine and radiator are cool to the touch.

2 Drain coolant from the radiator (see "Drain the Coolant" on page 56).

3 Remove the upper and lower radiator hoses.

4 If equipped, disconnect lines to the transmission cooler.

5 Detach electrical connections from the radiator cooling fan(s).

6 Remove the upper radiator support brackets.

7 Carefully lift the radiator up and away from the vehicle.

8 Remove the cooling fan(s) and shroud.

9 Take the radiator to a radiator repair shop or purchase a new or rebuilt radiator from an auto parts store.

10 Install the new radiator in reverse sequence.

FAQ

Should I use a radiator stop-leak product?
No!

Radiator stop-leak products work by distributing expanding material throughout the cooling system. While the material may stop a leak, it also may clog up jackets, ports, the thermostat, the heater core, and other components, making the problem worse.

If the radiator has a leak on the outside surface, consider using one of the external leak sealing products available at auto parts stores for temporary repair.

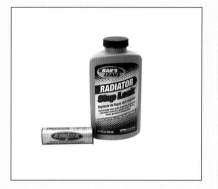

How the Lubrication System Works

Modern engines operate at up to 6,000 revolutions per minute (RPM)—that means the internal parts rotate 100 times every second! Without sufficient lubrication, the engine would wear out and stop within minutes. Fortunately, your car's lubrication works just as fast to keep parts from rubbing themselves to death.

Lubrication Systems 101

OIL

Engine oil (sometimes called motor oil) is a refined form of crude oil. It is an efficient lubricant. Chapter 2 describes how to select the correct oil for your vehicle. In addition to lubricating parts quickly, engine oil works as a heat exchanger that reduces internal engine heat. It also includes detergents that keep the engine cleaner to reduce friction and wear.

OIL PUMP

The *oil pump*'s job is to keep oil circulating in the engine and to make sure that all the appropriate parts are lubricated. If the oil pump doesn't work efficiently, oil may not get to some parts. Also, if the level of oil in the engine is low, some parts may not get sufficient lubrication and can wear out more quickly.

Lubrication System

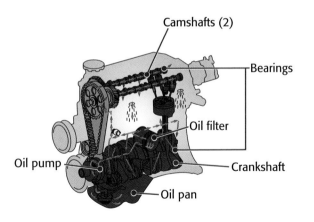

Camshafts (2)
Bearings
Oil filter
Oil pump
Crankshaft
Oil pan

Oil Pump Operation

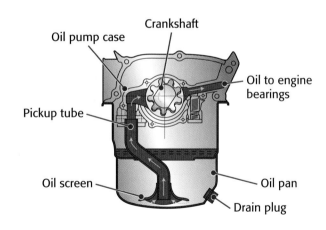

Crankshaft
Oil pump case
Oil to engine bearings
Pickup tube
Oil screen
Oil pan
Drain plug

TIP

When checking fluid levels—engine oil or transmission fluids—in your car, first make sure that the vehicle is level. If it isn't level, the reading will be inaccurate.

OIL FILTER

Because oil collects contaminants, it needs to be filtered constantly. As the oil flows through oil passages in the engine, it also flows through an *oil filter* that removes impurities (a cutaway of an oil filter is shown at right). Depending on driving conditions, the oil filter may need to be replaced sooner than standard mileage intervals. See Chapter 11 for service interval suggestions.

ENGINE BEARINGS

Within the engine, hundreds of parts move simultaneously. Many move more smoothly because they ride on movable metal bearings. These bearings are lubricated by oil as well. Damage to an engine bearing caused by insufficient oil lubrication can be very expensive to repair.

Other components of your car's lubrication system include the engine oil passages, oil seals and gaskets, the dipstick, and the oil pressure indicator.

Engine bearing

FAQ

What's the difference between an engine and a motor?

Though many people refer to the power plant in a car as the "motor," it really is the "engine." An *engine* is any machine that uses energy to develop mechanical power. A *motor* is a machine that converts electrical energy into mechanical energy. Your car's engine is started with a starter motor, for example. Now you know!

Change the Oil and Filter

Clean oil is critical to minimizing engine wear. Because changing the oil and filter in most cars is a relatively easy job, many owners make this their first maintenance project.

Drain the Oil

1 Make sure that the engine is cool to the touch.

2 Gather the parts and tools you need: oil, filter, funnel, drain plug wrench, filter wrench, oil collection pan, and rags. Your car's owner's manual will tell you how much oil you need and which filter to use.

3 Identify the location of the engine oil drain plug. Don't confuse it with the transmission fluid drain plug. If in doubt, check the owner's manual for the location on your specific car model.

4 Place the oil collection pan under the drain plug.

5 Loosen the drain plug (see close-up photo at right) with the drain plug wrench or an adjustable wrench.

6 Quickly remove the drain plug to keep the oil from splattering on you.

7 Allow the oil to drain completely.

8 Wipe the drain hole, plug, and threads with a clean rag.

9 Replace and tighten the drain plug.

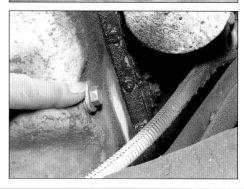

Change the Oil Filter

① Move the oil collection pan under the oil filter.

② Use a filter wrench to loosen and remove the oil filter. Note that it will contain oil.

③ Wipe off the oil filter sealing area on the engine block.

④ Apply a coating of clean engine oil on the new filter's seal.

⑤ Install the new oil filter (see photo at right) and hand-tighten it, following the instructions on the filter or the filter box.

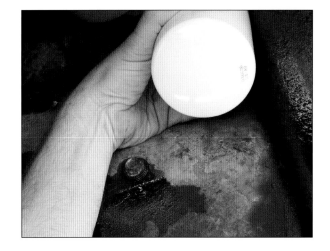

Refill the Oil

① In the engine compartment, remove the oil filler cap.

② Insert a funnel into the oil filler opening.

③ Carefully pour the recommended amount of oil into the funnel.

④ Replace the oil filler cap.

⑤ Start the engine to allow the oil to warm up and circulate through the filter. Meanwhile, visually inspect the filter and drain plug for leaks.

⑥ Check the oil level (refer to Chapter 3) to verify that it is within the normal operating range.

Note: Dispose of used oil following local regulations. Auto parts clerks can offer advice on oil disposal.

FAQ

How often should I change my car's oil and filter?

As frequently as is recommended by the manufacturer. In normal driving, many manufacturers recommend changing the oil and filter at intervals of about 3,000 to 5,000 miles. If you do a lot of stop-and-go driving or pull heavy loads, change them every 1,500 to 2,500 miles. The oil and filter for most cars cost less than $25. New engines cost thousands.

Service the Transmission

Thanks to the transmission, the engine doesn't work much harder going 65 mph than it does when moving at 25 mph. It uses internal gears, just like on a multispeed bicycle, to adjust the power delivered to the wheels.

Because the transmission distributes the engine's power to the wheels, transmission problems can stop your car in its tracks. Check fluid levels every three months, and plan to have the transmission serviced about every 30,000 miles.

Manual and Automatic Transmissions

GET TO KNOW AND SERVICE TRANSMISSIONS

A *manual transmission* enables you to select the gears that are used. An *automatic transmission* changes gears automatically, based on the design and an internal computer. A *transaxle* is simply a manual or automatic transmission and differential for front- and four-wheel-drive cars.

A *clutch* helps change manual transmission gears. A *torque converter* does the same for automatic transmissions.

MANUAL TRANSMISSION SERVICE

Manual transmissions are simpler in operation than automatic transmissions. However, they still need lubrication. To service a manual transmission, follow these steps:

1. Check your car's owner's manual for recommended service intervals. Many manufacturers suggest that manual transmission/transaxle gear oil be checked every 7,500 to 30,000 miles.

2. If your car's transmission is equipped with a dipstick, check the fluid level from the engine compartment. The transmission on a rear-wheel-drive car is behind the engine; on a front-wheel-drive car, it is next to the engine between the front wheels.

3. If your car's transmission doesn't have a dipstick, safely raise the car on a jack or hoist and remove the filler plug (see photo at right) on the side of the transmission. Lubrication should be within ½ inch of the hole.

4. Add manual transmission lubricant as needed.

AUTOMATIC TRANSMISSION SERVICE

Automatic transmissions are more complex than manual transmissions—and more sensitive to lubrication. Chapter 3 shows you how to check and add automatic transmission (AT) fluid. Here's how to change the fluid and filter:

1 Make sure that the engine and transmission are within normal operating temperatures. If they aren't, drive the car for five minutes before starting.

2 Safely jack up the car or put it on a garage rack for service.

3 Gather the parts and tools you need: AT fluid, filter, gasket, screwdriver, fluid collection pan, funnel, and rags. Your car's owner's manual will tell you how much AT fluid you need and which filter to use.

4 Place the fluid collection pan under the transmission.

5 If the transmission has one, remove the fluid drain plug. If not, remove the cover from the bottom of the transmission, following the instructions in the car's service manual.

6 Allow the transmission fluid to drain completely. If the cover is not off, remove it to replace the filter and inspect the transmission.

7 Replace the automatic transmission filter as recommended by the manufacturer.

8 Clean the transmission cover and inspect visible components for obvious wear or damage.

9 Reinstall the transmission cover with a *new* gasket.

10 Use a funnel to add recommended AT fluid through the fluid-check tube inside the engine compartment. Do not overfill.

11 Start the car, run it through the gears, and allow it to warm up.

12 Use the transmission dipstick to check the AT fluid level. Add fluid as needed.

TIP

A manual or automatic transaxle is simply a transmission combined with a differential (more gears). Service a transaxle unit as recommended by the manufacturer, typically the same as a manual or automatic transmission.

Use Lubricant on Other Moving Parts

Other moving parts in your car require lubrication, such as the differential and various fittings in the suspension system. In addition, other parts can benefit from periodic lubrication.

Lubricate the Differential, Fittings, and Other Components

CHECK THE DIFFERENTIAL FLUID

Rear-wheel-drive cars have a differential that splits the engine/transmission power between the two wheels. Transaxles combine the transmission and differential into a single unit. To check fluid in a differential, follow these steps:

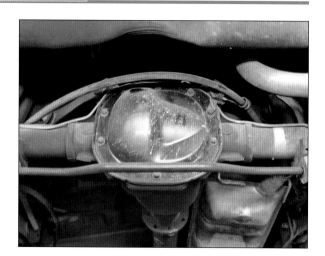

① Safely raise the car on a jack or hoist and remove the filler plug on the side of the differential case (see photo at right). Lubrication should be level with or within ½ inch of the hole.

② Add differential lubricant as recommended by the car's manufacturer. In most cases, the differential uses the same grease lubricant as a manual transmission.

LUBRICATE THE FITTINGS

Some modern cars have sealed components that cannot be lubricated. However, many cars still have grease fittings (called *zerk fittings*) into which lubricating grease can be forced under pressure. In most cases, these fittings are on the car's suspension system (see Chapter 7). Here's how to lubricate the fittings:

① Purchase a grease gun designed for zerk fittings. It should include a tube of lubricating grease.

② Wipe off the zerk fitting (see photo at right) to remove old grease and dirt on and around the fitting.

③ Press the grease gun tip to the zerk fitting and hold it firmly in place against the fitting.

④ Move the pressurizing lever to force grease into the fitting.

⑤ Stop inserting grease when you see excess grease exiting the component.

USE OTHER LUBRICANTS

With all the moving parts in a car, it's no wonder that things squeak, squeal, and wear out. Numerous automotive lubrication products can keep your car quieter longer.

- **WD-40** is the brand name of a penetrating oil that is useful for lubricating small moving parts.

- **Silicon spray** is a multipurpose product that lubricates, waterproofs, and reduces corrosion.

- **Graphite powder or spray** is a fine powder lubricant (sometimes in a base of light oil) for lubricating locks, bearings, and other very small parts.

- **Lithium grease** is a petroleum-based grease with lithium powder in it to enhance lubrication of larger moving parts.

- **Lightweight oil,** such as sewing machine oil, is a thin petroleum lubricant.

Make sure that you use the appropriate lubricant for the job. For example, lithium grease is popular for lubricating car door latches for smoother operation. Do not apply lubricants on or near electrical components.

chapter

Electrical

Gasoline and diesel vehicles need electricity to run. They need spark for the spark plugs (or glow for the diesel glow plugs), power for the starter and lights, and enough electricity to enable the computer, instruments, and safety devices to talk to each other. And they need an alternator to recharge the battery. This chapter explains how automotive electrical systems work and what you can specifically do to keep your car's system working.

How Electrical Systems Work

Electrical system components in your car include the battery, starter, alternator, spark plugs, ignition module, lighting, sound, computer, and sensors. Together, they control the power of your car.

Electrical Systems

Electricity is a source of power, and electronics are the components that put the power to work. Electricity and electronics go hand in hand to form the electrical system that powers your car. In these sections, I break down electrical systems into their major parts: electricity and electronics.

Electrical System

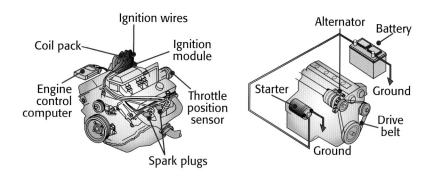

FAQ

How much do I have to know about electricity to safely work on it?

Not much. With a few exceptions, your car uses low-voltage devices that can shock you, but not hurt you. You'll typically be working on open, not closed, circuits, so no electricity is flowing. The greatest danger of electrical shock is from high-voltage coil and spark plug wires when the engine is running.

You will need to know a few basic terms. *Volt* is a measurement of power. Electricity being used is measured in *amperes* or *amps* of current. To do work, electricity must overcome resistance, measured in *ohms*. There's more to learn about automotive electricity in the next section, "Test Electrical Components."

ELECTRICITY 101

A car uses 12-volt direct current (DC) electricity for all of its electrical needs. The power is stored in the battery, which is recharged by the alternator when the engine is running. The battery's power turns the starter motor when needed and sends sparks to the spark plugs through the coil and ignition module or distributor.

All electricity requires a loop or circuit to operate. For example, a wire from the positive (+) side of the battery conducts energy to the starter or other device, and then it returns through a wire on the negative (–) side of the battery. A switch in the circuit turns it ON or OFF. In the case of an automobile starter, the ignition is the switch.

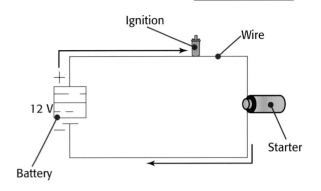

ELECTRONICS 101

Electronics are the components that do most of the thinking in a car. They are powered by electricity. Automotive electronics include semiconductors, integrated circuits, microprocessors, sensors, and similar devices. Fortunately, you don't have to work on them. Most are relatively trouble-free, and the ones that don't work can be replaced rather than repaired.

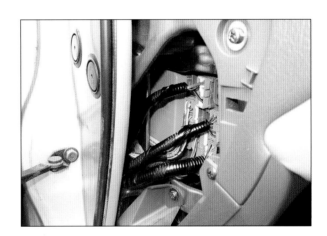

Subsystems

Within your car's electrical system are subsystems made up of codependent devices. They include the following:

- Battery and cables
- Starting system
- Charging system
- Lighting system
- Instrumentation
- Accessories

Each subsystem has a job to do. As you learn what that job is, you'll be able to diagnose problems and quickly solve them.

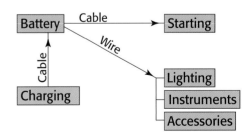

Test Electrical Components

Electricity works by the laws of physics. Most are logical. Electrical testers use these laws to report circuit conditions to you. Learn to use electrical testers, and you can take better care of your car. It's easy!

Use a Circuit Tester

Do NOT use a standard 12-volt circuit tester to diagnose components and wires in electrical systems. The battery inside the tester may be of higher voltage than the circuit and can damage components. Instead, purchase a circuit tester designed specifically for electronics.

Circuit testers identify open and shorted devices in electrical circuits by illuminating a light.

- *Non-powered testers* (no battery) are used to check whether voltage is available, such as at the posts of a car battery. These are used to test closed (ON) circuits.

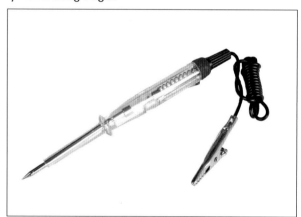

- *Self-powered testers* (internal battery) are used to check for continuity in a circuit or component, such as a light bulb. These are called *continuity testers* and are used to test open (OFF) circuits.

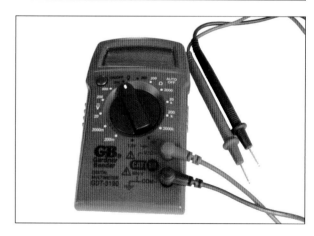

Use a Multimeter

A self-powered meter (internal battery) called a volt-ohmmeter, or *multimeter*, can test electrical volts (V), ohms (Ω), or amps (A) in a circuit or device. For example, to test the voltage level (drop) in an automotive battery, follow these steps:

1 Set the voltmeter section of the multimeter to its lowest DC (direct current) scale.

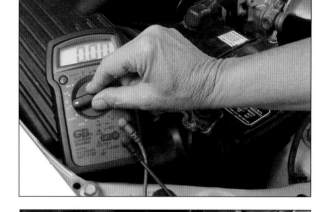

2 Connect the positive (red) lead to the positive (+) terminal post on the battery.

3 Connect the negative (black) lead to the negative (–) terminal post on the battery.

4 Read the voltage on the analog or digital scale.

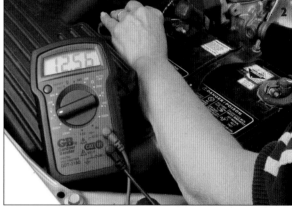

A *digital multimeter* (DMM) indicates the value as numbers on a digital display. An *analog multimeter* has a moving needle that indicates value on a printed scale. Read the multimeter manufacturer's instructions for more information and uses.

Read the Onboard Computer

Modern cars are controlled by onboard computers that monitor and adjust hundreds of settings for efficient operation. In addition, they also diagnose and report trouble in car systems. Fortunately, you can read the computer's trouble codes to maintain your car.

Check Trouble Codes on Older Vehicles

Older cars built before 1996 use proprietary code systems that report conditions as seen by the onboard computer. Refer to the owner's manual or repair manuals for the specific models to learn how to access and interpret these codes. In general:

- Chrysler vehicles have a logic module (LM) and power module (PM) system. To activate, turn the ignition key ON (*not* START) and OFF three times within five seconds, ending with it ON. Count the MIL (Check Engine) flashes, and refer to the manual to interpret the trouble codes.
- Ford vehicles have an EEC-IV diagnostic system, also accessed by turning the ignition key to ON (*not* START) and following steps to access the trouble codes. You need a manual to interpret the codes.
- General Motors vehicles use a Computer Command Control (CCC) diagnostic system accessed by turning the ignition to ON (*not* START) and following a troubleshooting chart.
- Nissan vehicles have a diagnostic setting on their computer that flashes light-emitting diodes (LEDs) in a pattern that can be interpreted by using the repair manual.
- Toyota vehicles have a proprietary system activated by turning the ignition key to ON (*not* START) and then connecting a jumper wire in the diagnostic link console (DLC) in the engine compartment.

Other manufacturers have similar systems for diagnosing onboard computer trouble codes.

Use an OBD-II Reader

Fortunately, major car manufacturers eventually got together and agreed on a standard for onboard diagnostic (OBD) systems and trouble codes. The first version was quickly replaced by the second, OBD-II, which has been the standard used in all new vehicles sold in North America since 1996. Various aftermarket products are available for auto mechanics as well as consumers (refer to Chapter 1). Consumer OBD-II diagnostic units can be purchased for less than $100 and can greatly simplify car care and maintenance. In addition, you can use one to verify that the information your mechanic is giving you is accurate.

There are four simple steps to using a consumer-level OBD-II diagnostic tool:

① Find the 16-pin data link connector (DLC) on your car. Most are located under the dashboard on the driver's side, but they can be in other places within reach of the driver.

② Plug the diagnostic tool into the connector. Within 10 seconds, turn the ignition key to the ON (*not* START) position.

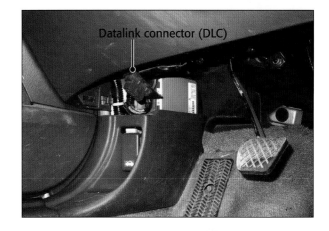

Datalink connector (DLC)

③ Wait for the data download to complete, usually within just a few seconds. Many units beep four times to report successful data retrieval.

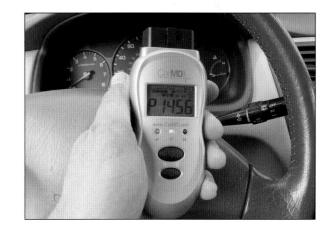

④ Refer to the tool's printed documentation, computer software, or website to decode the trouble codes, called PIDs (refer to Chapter 1). Most reports include an error code and error name, define the condition, and list the possible causes. Some websites also offer estimates of repair costs and even recommend nearby mechanics.

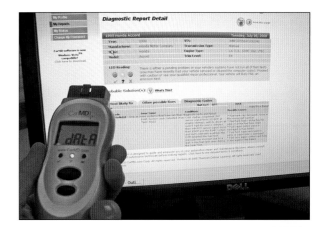

Replace the Battery

Where would your car be without a battery? Parked. The starter needs electricity to start the engine. Once it's running, the engine replaces electricity in the battery so it can be used for other functions—and to start the car again.

Check, Find, and Install a Battery

Modern car batteries have a typical life span of four to six years, depending on quality, care, and use. If you take a few minutes every month to check and clean the battery (refer to Chapter 3), you can extend its life. However, if you find that your car is in need of a new battery, you need to select one and then install it.

TEST THE BATTERY

To test the voltage in an automotive battery, refer to "Use a Multimeter," on page 73.

If the battery has filler caps on the top, you can use a battery hydrometer (available at auto parts stores) to test the condition of the electrolyte inside, following the instructions available with the instrument.

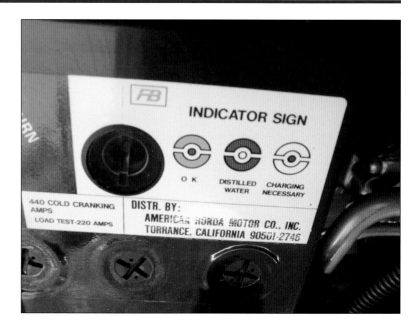

If it is a maintenance-free battery, view the built-in hydrometers on top of the battery to determine its state of charge. The tester looks like a round eye on top of the battery. If there is a green dot in the center of the eye, the cells are 65 percent or above a full state of charge. If the eye is dark, without a dot in the center, the battery is below a full state of charge. If the eye is clear, the electrolyte is low. There is no way to refill the electrolyte in a maintenance-free battery; you will need to recharge or replace the battery.

SELECT A BATTERY

In most cases, selecting a new car battery is as easy as identifying the current battery and buying another one that's just as good or better. However, before you do, check the owner's manual to make sure that the current battery is the one recommended by the car manufacturer.

- Select a replacement battery with at least a 60-month warranty from a reputable source that will honor the warranty.
- Make sure that the replacement is of the correct group number and size recommended by the manufacturer.
- Make sure that the battery terminals are in the same location as the old battery, either on the top or on the sides.
- Batteries are rated by cold-crank amps (CCA). Buy the highest CCA rating available within your budget.

INSTALL THE BATTERY

Replacing a battery is an easy job, though it can be dangerous if you are careless. Wear eye protection and be careful not to drop the battery. In addition, make sure you read the owner's manual for any cautions about protecting the computer and the air bag system (see the tip at the bottom of this page).

1 Open the car's hood and locate the battery.

2 Disconnect the black cable from the negative (–) terminal and then the red cable from the positive (+) terminal.

3 Remove the bracket or frame holding the battery in place.

4 Carefully lift the battery out of the engine compartment and set it down.

5 Inspect the cable terminals for corrosion or damage. If necessary, replace them with cables of the same type (black or red) and length.

6 Clean the cable terminals with a wire battery brush (available at auto parts stores) and a paste of baking soda and water to neutralize acid on the surface.

7 Use a wire battery brush to clean the terminals of the new battery for better contact.

8 Connect the red cable to the positive battery terminal, connect the black cable to the negative battery terminal, and then tighten both.

9 Start the engine to test the battery installation.

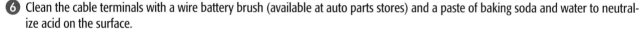

TIP

Warning

Your car's battery is the sole source of electrical power for all of its systems, including the computer, radio, and air bags. Make sure you read the owner's manual for cautions about disconnecting and removing the battery. You can damage the computer, lose the security code for the radio, or inadvertently activate air bags. Each is an expensive error.

Replace the Starter

Your car's starter motor has an important job: to turn the engine until it can power itself. The job takes only a few seconds at the beginning of each trip, but the trip won't start until the starter does.

Test and Replace the Starter and Relay

An electric starter turns the engine when it begins operating. The *relay* delivers electricity from the battery to the starter. Like other car components, starter motors and relays aren't repaired—even by most mechanics. They are replaced. Here's how to test and replace a starter motor, as well as how to replace the relay.

TEST THE STARTER MOTOR

To perform an electrical test on a starter motor, you need a multimeter and a remote starter switch.

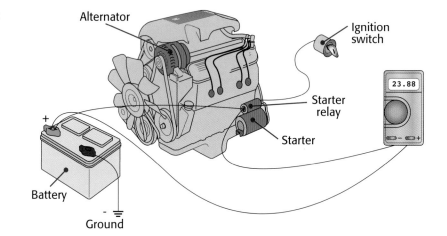

1. Connect the positive lead of the meter to the positive battery post.

2. Connect the negative lead of the meter to the main battery connection at the starter, located at the bottom rear of the engine.

3. Set the DC Volt section of the multimeter to the 10–20V scale.

4. Connect and use the remote starter switch as recommended by the tool manufacturer, bypassing the ignition. The voltage reading should be approximately the battery voltage (12–14V).

5. Move the negative lead to the starter side of the starter relay (a small component near the battery).

6. Use the remote starter to check voltage coming from the starter relay. It should be approximately the same as the battery.

7. Move the negative lead to the battery side of the starter relay and use the remote starter to check voltage. Again, it should be the same as the battery.

8. Electrical voltage readings should be the same at all points between the battery and the starter. A dramatic voltage drop indicates the location of the problem component. If voltage at the starter is the same as the battery, replace the starter.

REPLACE THE STARTER RELAY

To replace the starter relay, follow these steps:

Note: *Some starter relays are mounted on the starter.*

1. Disconnect the negative cable on the battery, noting the *Warning* tip under "Replace the Battery" on page 77.

2. Remove the cable between the starter relay and the battery.

3. Remove the cable between the starter relay and the starter motor.

4. Remove the starter relay, typically bolted to the compartment side wall.

5. Install the new starter relay (available at auto parts stores), reversing the steps you took to remove the old unit.

6. Install the cable between the relay and the battery and between the relay and the starter.

7. Reconnect the negative cable on the battery and start the engine.

REPLACE THE STARTER MOTOR

To replace the starter motor (shown in photo at right), follow these steps:

1. Disconnect the negative cable on the battery, noting the *Warning* tip under "Replace the Battery" on page 77.

2. Remove the cable between the starter relay and the starter motor.

3. From under the car, remove the two bolts that attach the starter to the engine.

4. Install the new starter motor (available at auto parts stores) on the engine.

5. Install the cable between the relay and the starter.

6. Reconnect the negative cable on the battery and start the engine.

Replace the Alternator

An automotive alternator generates alternating current, so it's technically known as an AC generator. Most folks call it an alternator. An *alternator* replaces current in the battery used by the starter and other electrical components. Alternators are relatively easy to test and to replace.

Test the Alternator

To perform an electrical test on an alternator, you need a multimeter.

1 Make sure that the engine is not running and the ignition is in the OFF position.

2 Set the DC Volt section of the multimeter to the 10–20V scale.

3 Connect the positive lead of the meter to the positive battery post.

4 Connect the negative lead of the meter to the negative battery post.

5 Read the voltage with the engine off. It should be 12–13V. If lower, the battery should be recharged.

6 Turn the ignition on and start the engine.

7 Read the voltage with the engine running. It should be 13–15V. If lower, the alternator is not working. Check all connections and wires. If the alternator output to the battery still isn't within the normal range, consider replacing the alternator.

Note: *Before purchasing a new alternator, remove the old alternator and take it to an auto parts store for more accurate testing. Call ahead to find out if they can test your alternator.*

Replace the Alternator

To replace the alternator:

1 First, locate the alternator. If you're not sure you've properly identified the alternator, check the car's repair manual for its specific location.

2 Disconnect the negative cable on the battery, noting the *Warning* tip under "Replace the Battery" on page 77.

3 Loosen the alternator belt adjustment with a wrench and remove the alternator drive belt. Some models use an automatic tensioner to maintain the correct tension on the belt.

4 Disconnect all wires and wiring harness clips to and from the alternator. If necessary, mark them for easier installation later.

5 Remove the bolts securing the alternator to the engine and any brackets. Remove the alternator.

6 Install the new alternator on the engine and brackets.

7 Inspect the drive belt (refer to Chapter 3). If it's worn, replace the belt.

8 Tighten the alternator belt adjustment or reinstall the automatic tensioner.

9 Reconnect the negative cable on the battery.

10 Test the alternator output, per the instructions on the previous page.

FAQ

Should I buy a new or rebuilt alternator or starter?

Who do you trust? If you're concerned about the quality of aftermarket parts, purchase OEM (original-equipment manufacturer) parts. If you trust your auto parts store to stand behind what it sells, consider a rebuilt unit. Rebuilt parts typically cost 60 to 75 percent that of new parts. Don't install cheap parts, or you may be doing it again.

Replace Spark Plugs

Each engine spark plug makes high-voltage electricity jump between two surfaces, producing a spark. The spark ignites a compressed gasoline-and-air mixture in a combustion chamber. The resulting combustion rotates engine components to eventually turn the wheels. Because spark plugs wear out, they are replaceable. It's an easy job.

Check and Install Spark Plugs

CHECK SPARK PLUG CONDITION

Check the condition of your spark plugs as recommended by the car manufacturer. Many manufacturers recommend replacing spark plugs every one to two years (15,000 to 30,000 miles), though high-performance spark plugs can operate well for up to 100,000 miles before being replaced. In many cars you can do the job yourself if you have the basic tools (refer to Chapter 2).

Spark plugs are screwed tightly into an engine. There is one spark plug for each cylinder; for example, a four-cylinder engine has four spark plugs.

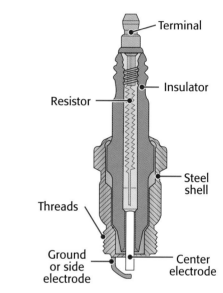

Here's how to check the condition of your spark plugs:

1. Make sure that the engine is cool to the touch.

2. Locate the spark plugs. On four-cylinder engines, they typically are on top of the engine, connected to a central point (ignition module) by individual spark plug wires. In V-6 and V-8 engines, the spark plugs may be on the engine sides near the top. Follow the wires from the ignition module.

3. Remove the wire from one spark plug cap. (Spark plug wires must be installed in the same position as they were removed.)

4. Use a spark plug socket wrench (available at auto parts stores) to remove the spark plug, turning counterclockwise. Automotive spark plugs are either 14mm or 18mm (more common) in size.

5. Inspect the spark plug tip for damage or excessive oil buildup. If you are in doubt of its condition, take the plug to an auto parts store for advice.

6. If a spark plug is damaged or has met or exceeded the recommended service life, replace all as a set.

BUY REPLACEMENT PLUGS

Before buying replacement spark plugs, check the owner's manual for recommendations. Engines are designed to operate with a specific type and size of plug. Using the wrong plug can damage your engine. The new plug doesn't have to be the same brand, but it must have the same specifications:

- Size (14mm or 18mm)
- Reach (how deep it goes into the combustion chamber)
- Heat range (hot or cold, per the engine manufacturer's recommendation)
- Resistor type (minimizes electrical interference between the spark plug and the car's electronics and radio)

For best results, take a sample plug to an auto parts store along with the engine manufacturer's recommended replacement part number.

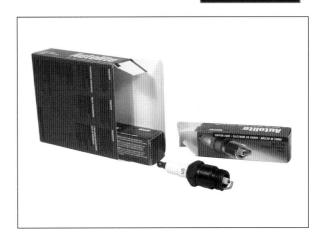

Note: The electrodes in a spark plug range in quality and cost from low (copper) to medium (platinum) to high (iridium) to highest (yttrium).

INSTALL SPARK PLUGS

New spark plugs are relatively easy to install in most cars. Here's how to do it:

1. Make sure that the engine is cool to the touch.
2. Remove the wire from one spark plug cap and remove the plug.
3. Use a spark plug gap tool to set the distance between the two electrodes (per the car's owner's manual).
4. Apply copper anti-seize compound to the spark plug threads to make future removal easier.
5. Carefully insert the new spark plug into the engine hole.
6. Make sure that the spark plug is seated in the hole, and then use a spark plug socket wrench to firmly tighten the plug. Overtightening the plug can break it.
7. Replace the spark plug wire. If in doubt on how to do this, refer to the owner's manual.

   Note: When replacing plugs, consider simultaneously testing cylinder compression (see Chapter 9).

Replace the Ignition Module

Until about 1984, cars used a mechanical distributor system to distribute spark to the plugs in the engine's firing order sequence. Modern cars have ignition modules (IM) to do this job, which are more efficient and last longer. There are no individual parts; if the IM goes bad, replace it.

Test the Ignition Module

The *ignition module* controls the delivery of high-voltage sparks to the spark plugs. A component called the *ignition coil* converts 12 volts into 30,000 to 60,000 volts needed by the plugs. Older cars used a single coil for the engine; modern cars typically have more than one ignition coil.

The IM controls these sparks. Inside the IM are triggering and switching devices that send the sparks to the appropriate spark plugs and cylinders.

Testing an electronic IM requires special diagnostic equipment. Some troubleshooting charts (in your car's repair manual) may indicate that the solution to a problem is to replace the IM. Your ODB-II module may also suggest IM replacement. If so, consider doing the job yourself. Refer to the simplified instructions on the following page, or to more specific instructions in your car's repair manual.

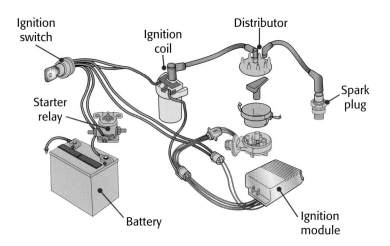

Install the Ignition Module

Purchase an exact replacement ignition module. Most auto parts stores can help you identify the location of the IM and make recommendations on how best to remove the unit for replacement. Following is the installation process for a common IM unit:

1 Disconnect the negative cable on the battery, noting the *Warning* tip under "Replace the Battery" on page 77.

2 Remove the distributor cap, ignition rotor, and protective cover.

3 Detach the wires from the IM and remove the unit.

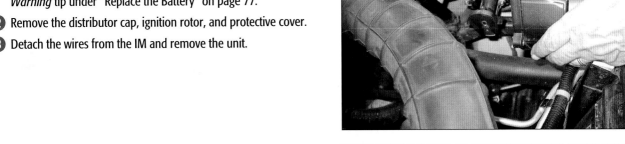

4 Install the new IM and reattach the wires.

5 Replace the protective cover, rotor, and cap.

6 Reconnect the negative cable on the battery.

TIP

Distributor Repair

In an effort to increase fuel economy and reduce pollutants, car manufacturers have made many design changes to ignition distributors over the past two decades. In addition, each manufacturer has developed its own proprietary system. If you are working on your car's ignition system, refer to the manufacturer's service manual for specific repair procedures.

Replace Light Bulbs

Automotive light bulbs, or lamps, are everywhere in your car. They illuminate the road ahead and signal turns and stops to the vehicles behind you. They also make instruments easier to read at night.

A lamp generates light as electrical current flows through a filament. Some lamps have a glass bulb and a single filament; others have two filaments encased in a gas-filled glass chamber. As with most car components, lamps are replaced rather than repaired.

Replace Exterior Lamps

Exterior lamps include headlights and rear exterior light assemblies. To replace headlights and rear lights, follow these steps:

1 Identify the type and access method.

- Composite headlights have a replaceable halogen bulb or high-intensity discharge (HID) xenon (blue-white) bulb, accessed from behind the housing. Most clip or screw in from the rear and are mounted in an electrical connector.

- Rear lights often use replaceable bulbs accessed from the rear of the housing (see photo at right). Many have either multiple bulbs or multiple filaments.

- Some cars use light-emitting diodes (LEDs) for rear brake lights and turn signal lights.

2 Identify the model and part number, typically engraved on the bulb or the lamp housing. Alternately, refer to the owner's manual.

FAQ

How can I figure out my car's lighting system?

Auto manufacturers offer a wiring diagram for all electrical systems in their cars, including the lighting system. You can find it in the car's authorized repair manual. The diagram can show you what lamps your car has and how they are powered and controlled, but it doesn't tell you where they are located.

Replace Interior Lamps

Your car's interior may have numerous lamps to illuminate the passenger compartment, instrument panel, glove box interior, vanity, engine compartment, and trunk. Eventually, the filament will burn out in a lamp and you'll need to replace it. Here's how:

1 Identify the access method. Most interior lights fit into sockets and are held in place by spring tension or mechanical force.

2 Remove the screws holding the cover in place.

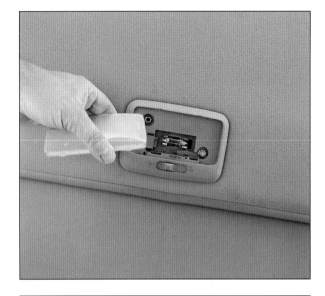

3 Read the bulb code numbers on the base. If in doubt, take the bulb to an auto parts store for reference.

4 Install the new bulb and replace the cover. If the bulb does not illuminate, check the circuit fuse (see "Replace Fuses" on the next page).

Code number

Replace Fuses

Fuses are designed to be the weakest link in an electrical chain. If problems occur in a fused circuit, the fuse fails first. Fortunately, most automotive circuits have fuses in them, and they are easy to check and replace.

Test and Replace Fuses

Most cars use either a blade fuse or a cartridge fuse. Both are easy to test and replace. If an electrical component quits working, test the fuse. If it fails the test, replace the fuse.

TEST A FUSE

To test an automotive fuse, follow these steps:

1. Remove the fuse from the holder.

2. Use a continuity tester or multimeter (see "Test Electrical Components" on pages 72–73) to test for continuity.

3. If the fuse fails the continuity test, replace it.

Blade fuses

Cartridge fuse

Mini-fuse

REPLACE A FUSE

Most automotive fuses are mounted together in a fuse box or panel. Here's how to replace a fuse:

1. Identify the correct fuse. Most fuse panels (see photo at right) have a map on the lid to help you identify fuses for specific systems. Some fuse panels also include a fuse puller tool.

2. Replace the fuse with one of the same voltage and amperage. Fuses have their amp rating printed on the case. Most automotive fuses are rated for 12 volts. Maximum amperage ratings include 4 (pink), 5 (tan), 10 (red), 15 (light blue), 20 (yellow), 25 (clear), 30 (light green), 40 (amber), 50 (red), and 60 (blue) amps.

   Note: Some cars also have a fuse and relay box mounted in the engine compartment for larger-circuit protective devices.

Wiring is the road that electricity takes to its destinations. The amount of electricity a wire can carry is identified by the American Wire Gauge (AWG) numbering system, which ranges from 0 to 20. Most automotive wiring ranges in size from 10 to 18 AWG. The smaller the number, the more electricity a wire can safely carry.

Test and Fix Wiring

You may never need to replace automotive wiring, but you may need to check for loose wires or terminals. If you suspect a wiring problem, check to make sure that the wiring harnesses and terminals are firmly connected. Once you're certain that the device is OFF, trace the connecting wire that may be faulty. If a connection is loose, carefully reconnect or move the terminals to make electrical contact.

TIP

Printed Circuit Boards

Printed circuit boards are simply wiring harnesses that are etched on to a non-conductive board. In addition, the boards may contain electronic components such as resistors. Like most other automotive parts, if a printed circuit board goes out, replace it—don't try to repair it.

chapter 6

Fuel

Fuel is a necessity to the operation of your car. It's also expensive. To help make sure that you get to where you're going, you must take good care of your car's fuel system. This chapter shows you how your fuel system works, what can go wrong, what to do when fuel system components need to be replaced, and how to keep your fuel system operating smoothly and efficiently.

How Fuel Systems Work

Internal combustion engines require two things: fuel and fire. The fuel system provides the gasoline and air mixture. The electrical system (refer to Chapter 5) provides the spark that lights the fire. The engine compresses the mixture and adds the spark, and controlled combustion powers the car.

Put the right fuel in your car, perform regular maintenance, and the fuel system is relatively trouble-free.

Fuel System Basics

The function of your car's fuel system is to deliver the amount of fuel needed for efficient operation. It's mixed with air, delivered to the engine, and then injected into the individual cylinders.

Fuel System

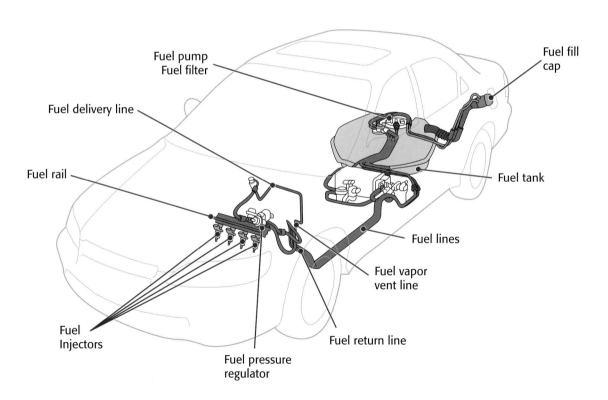

Fuel pump
Fuel filter

Fuel fill cap

Fuel delivery line

Fuel rail

Fuel tank

Fuel lines

Fuel vapor vent line

Fuel Injectors

Fuel return line

Fuel pressure regulator

FUEL/AIR MIXTURE

For every gallon of gasoline fuel your car burns, it needs to be mixed with nearly 10,000 gallons of air. If there is less air per gallon of fuel, the mixture is *rich;* if there is more air per gallon of fuel, the mixture is *lean.* Fuel efficiency and pollution standards require that the mixture be efficient. That's why your car's brain (computer) constantly analyzes and controls the fuel/air mixture.

Gasoline, jet fuel, diesel, heating oil, wax, lubricants, and asphalt are all products of the refining of crude oil. As illustrated below, gasoline is more refined than jet fuel, jet fuel is more refined than diesel fuel, and so on. Chemicals are added to the gas for better performance and cleaner burning. For many years, the primary additive was tetraethyl lead (called *ethyl*), now removed for environmental reasons. Today's gas is unleaded and includes other chemicals to keep engine components clean. Octane ratings are discussed in Chapter 1 in the section "Gas Station Wisdom."

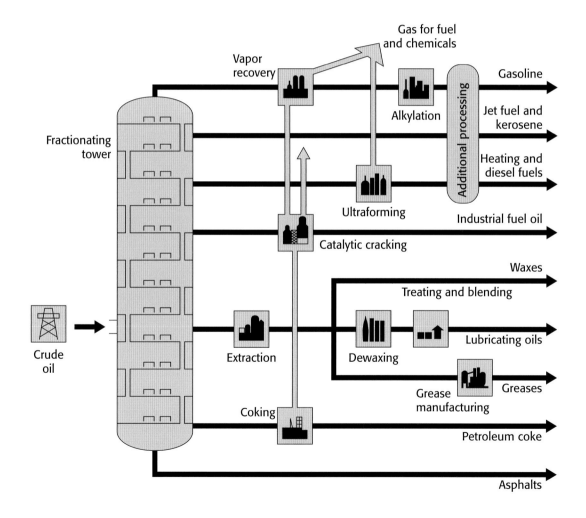

CONTINUED ON NEXT PAGE

FUEL DELIVERY

Gasoline is stored in your car's fuel tank awaiting delivery to the engine by a fuel pump. An inline filter traps sediments that can clog small passageways and ports. Fuel lines carry the fuel to the engine. (Refer to the "Fuel System" illustration on page 92.)

FUEL INJECTION

In the 1980s, car manufacturers replaced inefficient carburetors with fuel injection systems. Electronic fuel injection (EFI) systems monitor and adjust the amounts of fuel and air for greatest engine efficiency. Modern cars use numerous devices in the fuel system, including the following:

- Throttle position (TP) sensor
- Manifold absolute pressure (MAP) sensor
- Intake air temperature (IAT) sensor
- Cylinder position (CYP) sensor

- Vehicle speed sensor (VSS)
- Engine coolant temperature (ECT) sensor
- Knock sensor (KS)

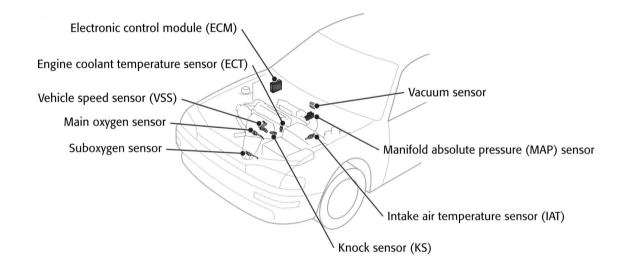

Electronic control module (ECM)

Engine coolant temperature sensor (ECT)

Vehicle speed sensor (VSS)

Main oxygen sensor

Suboxygen sensor

Vacuum sensor

Manifold absolute pressure (MAP) sensor

Intake air temperature sensor (IAT)

Knock sensor (KS)

TIP

Alternative Fuels

Cars can also be powered by diesel fuel, liquefied petroleum gas (LPG), compressed natural gas (CNG), ethanol, electricity, fuel cells, or a combination of two of these, called a *hybrid*. Some fuels, such as ethanol, can run in newer gasoline cars with no problems. Fuels such as LPG require simple conversions of gasoline engines. Others, such as diesel, use similar designs, but not the same engines. Newer fuel sources require new designs for modern cars.

Fuel is relatively pure when it leaves the refinery. However, from sitting in a tank farm to traveling in a truck tank, being pumped into underground tanks, and finally being pumped into your car's tank, it can collect particles and other contaminants that can damage the engine. The job of the *fuel filter* is to remove these contaminants before they reach the fuel injectors and other sensitive components.

Steps to Replace the Fuel Filter

Modern cars have a variety of fuel filtering systems. Some are designed to allow fuel filter replacement every year or two with basic tools. Others are built to last the lifetime of the car and are very difficult to replace.

1. LOCATE THE FUEL FILTER

Automotive fuel filters should be replaced (not cleaned), as specified by the car manufacturer, typically every 15,000 to 30,000 miles. Check the owner's manual for specific service recommendations.

The fuel filter may be located anywhere between your car's fuel tank and the fuel injectors. Some are installed with the fuel pump inside the fuel tank. Others are located under the car somewhere along the path of the fuel lines. The filter may also be in the engine compartment. Check the owner's manual or service manual for location and procedures.

2. DEPRESSURIZE THE FUEL SYSTEM

Older, carbureted cars relied on the engine to pull fuel into the combustion chamber. Fuel-injected cars use a pressurized fuel system. For safety, fuel systems must be depressurized before any work can be performed, including replacing a fuel filter. Refer to your car's repair manual for specific instructions. In general, here are the steps:

1 Disconnect the negative cable of the battery.

2 Loosen the fuel tank filler cap to relieve pressure in the tank.

3 Loosen the service bolt (the Schrader valve) on the fuel rail to relieve pressure in the fuel lines.

4 Replace the fuel filter.

CONTINUED ON NEXT PAGE

3. REPLACE THE FUEL FILTER

Fuel filters typically are cylindrical metal or plastic parts with an inlet and outlet connector. Filtration is accomplished by passing the fuel through folds of porous paper inside. To install a new filter, follow these steps:

1 Remove the old filter. Many are installed inline with the fuel line using clips over the inlet and outlet.

2 Select the correct replacement filter, available at auto parts stores. Use the part number printed on the filter.

3 Identify the fuel flow direction, typically marked on the outside of the filter.

4 Install the new filter with flow in the correct direction.

5 Reinstall clips or other fasteners to seal the connections.

TIP

One of the most common OBD-II diagnostic codes relates to the fuel fill cap. If your car's CHECK ENGINE light comes on, especially after you just filled up the tank, check the cap to make sure that it is firmly twisted in place, sealing the pressurized tank. If the problem repeats, replace the fuel fill cap.

The fuel pump pulls fuel from the tank with sufficient pressure to deliver it to the engine. Modern cars use electric fuel pumps that are replaced rather than repaired.

Steps to Replace the Fuel Pump

If your car's engine doesn't seem to be getting enough fuel, the fuel pump may be faulty. To replace the fuel pump, follow these steps:

1. LOCATE THE FUEL PUMP

The fuel pump can be located anywhere between the fuel tank and the engine. In older cars with mechanical pumps, the pump is installed on the engine. Most modern car manufacturers install the fuel pump in or near the fuel tank.

When should you replace the fuel pump? Because you don't know when it will fail, consider the mileage and age of the car, the ease of replacement, and the cost—especially if you already are replacing a fuel filter located with the fuel pump. You don't have to wait for a failure before replacing the pump.

2. DEPRESSURIZE THE FUEL SYSTEM

When you replace components in modern fuel systems, you must first depressurize the system. See "Depressurize the Fuel System" on page 95 and refer to your car's service manual for specifics.

3. INSTALL THE FUEL PUMP

To install a fuel pump located in the fuel tank, follow these steps:

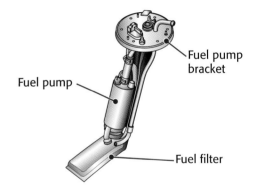

Fuel pump bracket

Fuel pump

Fuel filter

❶ Check the car trunk for an access plate in the floor. You may be able to remove the plate to get to the top of the fuel tank and access the fuel pump.

❷ If you cannot access the fuel pump through the trunk floor, refer to the car's service manual for instructions to lower the fuel tank and access the fuel pump.

❸ Disconnect the negative cable of the battery.

❹ Disconnect the electrical connections to the fuel pump.

❺ Disconnect the fuel lines.

❻ Remove the fuel pump.

❼ Install the new pump in reverse order.

To install a fuel pump located outside of the fuel tank, follow these steps:

❶ Disconnect the negative cable of the battery.

❷ Disconnect the electrical connections to the fuel pump.

❸ Disconnect the fuel lines.

❹ Remove the fuel pump.

❺ Install the new pump in reverse order.

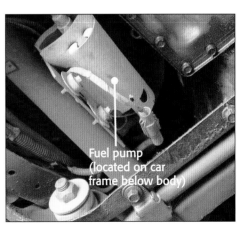

Fuel pump (located on car frame below body)

The fuel lines in your car deliver the fuel from the car's tank to the engine. There are no moving parts, so they don't wear out. However, they can become brittle with age, pressure, and the constant flow of fuel. You can replace them.

Inspect and Install Fuel Lines

Those spots on the garage floor may be caused by a leaking fuel system, specifically a damaged fuel line. Wearing rubber gloves, touch the liquid and then smell it. If it smells like gasoline, inspect the underside of the car to find the source. It may be a bad fuel line.

If you suspect that there is a fuel leak from a pressurized fuel system, refer the problem to a mechanic who will have the equipment to pressure-check the system. If you know where the leak is and feel comfortable replacing the problem line, you'll need to depressurize the fuel system before installing the new lines.

Follow these steps for inspecting and replacing fuel lines:

1. FIND THE FUEL LINES

Fuel system lines serve different functions. Some carry fuel to the engine. Others allow fuel to return to the tank. Still others serve to vent vapors safely. All lines in an automotive fuel system are manufactured for their specific application.

Fuel lines typically run from the top of the fuel tank, along one of the car's frame rails, forward to the engine area, and connect to the fuel rail that distributes fuel to the fuel injectors. (See illustration on page 92.) They are made of metal tubing, flexible nylon, or flexible synthetic rubber hose. Longer spans of fuel line, such as the ones that run from near the tank to near the engine, are made of metal tubing. Near the engine and the fuel tank, flexible lines are used to absorb vibrations.

Fittings connect the lines together at various points, such as from a flexible line to a rigid one. Fittings on rigid lines are threaded, like pipes. Flexible lines use quick-disconnect fittings that are rotated to unlock. An internal O-shaped ring makes the seal.

2. EXAMINE THE FUEL LINES

While most fuel lines are made of rubber, neoprene, or other soft materials, fuel lines near the engine are made of metal because of the heat. Trace and examine fuel lines for cracks or other damage. Also look at connections to make sure they are tight. If necessary, replace the fuel line.

3. DEPRESSURIZE THE FUEL SYSTEM

When replacing components in modern fuel systems, you must first depressurize the system. See "Depressurize the Fuel System" on page 95 and refer to your car's service manual for specifics.

4. INSTALL FUEL LINES

When replacing any fuel line, make sure that the replacement is one of similar construction and size.

- Replace steel tubing with steel tubing of the same rating, diameter, and length. Do not use aluminum or copper tubing to replace steel tubing in fuel systems.
- Replace flexible tubing with nylon or synthetic rubber tubing of the same rating, diameter, and length.
- Do not install flexible tubing within 4 inches of any engine or exhaust system component that can become hot. Use metal tubing for these installations.

To make a replacement fuel line, follow these steps:

1 Select the correct type, diameter, and length of replacement line.

2 Cut the line slightly longer than the old line.

3 If the line is metal, use a tube bender to shape the line, using the old line as a pattern. Don't attempt to make sharp bends by hand.

4 For metal lines, use a flaring tool (shown below at right; available at auto parts stores) to make the end connections, following the tool manufacturer's instructions.

5 Replace the end fittings with new, identical fittings.

Replace the Fuel Injector

Modern cars inject fuel under pressure into combustion chambers. Most have a fuel injector at each cylinder port, hence the name port fuel injection (PFI). Fuel injectors, like most automotive parts, can be replaced with basic tools on most cars.

Fuel Injection 101

Fuel injectors are devices that meter out a specific amount of fuel to each cylinder, as directed by the powertrain control module (PCM). The injectors also atomize the fuel into a fine spray for more efficient ignition.

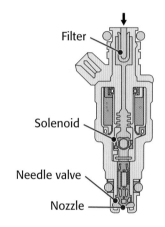

Modern cars are much more efficient than older models because the fuel mixture and spark are precisely controlled in each individual combustion chamber. Sensors monitor engine inputs and outputs to keep everything running as designed. The result is better fuel mileage and lower emissions in modern cars.

Install Fuel Injectors

Make sure that the new fuel injectors are exact replacements required by the car manufacturer. If in doubt, take an old fuel injector and the car model information (refer to Chapter 2) to your auto parts supplier.

For specific instructions on removing and replacing fuel injectors on your car, refer to the service manual. In general, to replace a fuel injector in a PFI fuel system (other systems are similar) follow these steps:

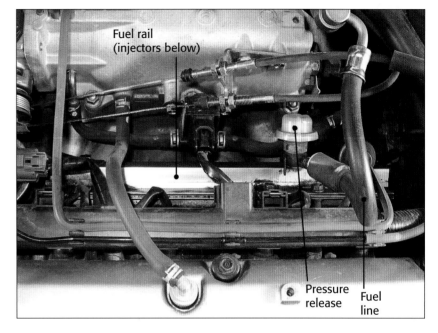

Fuel rail
(injectors below)

Pressure release

Fuel line

1 Disconnect the negative cable of the battery. Alternately, remove the fuel pump fuse from the fuse box (refer to Chapter 5).

2 Unbolt the brackets holding the fuel rail to the engine.

3 Disconnect the vacuum line to the pressure regulator.

4 Disconnect the wire harness to the injectors. Some models have a wire clip that must be depressed to release the harness.

5 Lift the fuel rail assembly to pull the injectors out of the manifold.

6 Remove the clip from the top of the injector.

7 Remove the injector.

8 Install the new fuel injector with a new O-ring.

9 Install the injector into the fuel rail.

10 Set the fuel rail back into place.

11 Reinstall the brackets and vacuum line.

12 Reconnect the negative battery cable or reinstall the fuel pump fuse.

Modern cars are more fuel efficient, in part because there are numerous sensors that report conditions to the car's powertrain control module (PCM). Your car probably has more than a dozen such sensors, each designed for a specific task. If OBD-II troubleshooting tells you that a sensor has failed, you probably can replace it—if you can find it.

Locate Sensors

Fuel injection system sensors are used to control the air/fuel mixture. Airflow sensors measure the amount and temperature of air entering the engine. A mass airflow sensor is mounted on the air intake near the front of the engine compartment. A vane airflow sensor measures air volume at the engine's intake, called the manifold. Some systems have a separate air temperature sensor. Other systems have a manifold absolute pressure (MAP) sensor instead of the other airflow sensors.

In addition, many cars have separate sensors for oxygen, coolant temperature, throttle position, emissions, engine speed, altitude compensation, crankshaft position, and other functions.

Throttle position sensor

Emission sensor

To find and replace sensors on your car, you need a map. The car's service manual includes diagrams to help you locate specific sensors, as well as instructions on how to replace them.

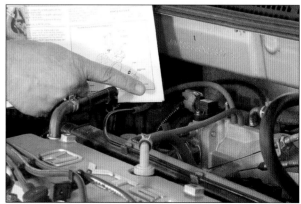

Replace Sensors

Because there are a wide variety of sensors, there are many ways to remove and replace them.

Note: Before removing any sensor, check the car's service manual for safety warnings. Some automotive systems are pressurized. Others are closed electrical circuits with live voltage electronics. Some have hot coolant in them. Work safely!

General steps for replacing auto system sensors are given below, by type:

- **Plug-in sensors (a):** Unclip the wiring harness connections, remove the sensor, install the new one, and plug it in.
- **Screw-in sensors (b):** Loosen the sensor with a wrench, remove the sensor, and install the new sensor.
- **In-line sensors (c):** Loosen or unclip the connections at both ends, remove the sensor, and install the new sensor.

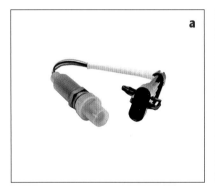
a

b

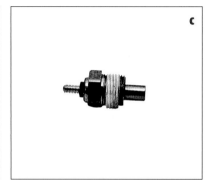
c

TIP

Buying Sensors

Sensors are small electronic devices that produce a signal that your engine relies on to work efficiently. Make sure that you get the *exact replacement* sensor rather than a generic one. The wrong sensor can confuse the PCM and make operation difficult or impossible. If necessary, remove the sensor and take it to your auto parts supplier to get an exact replacement.

Replace the Air Filter

As mentioned earlier in this chapter, your car needs nearly 10,000 gallons of air for every gallon of gas it burns. The air comes into the engine compartment through an intake duct. To keep road dust and bugs out of the engine, cars have replaceable air filters.

Know When to Replace the Air Filter

How frequently should you replace the air filter? As needed. Most car manufacturers recommend replacing it once a year. If you put more than 15,000 miles on your car in a year or drive through dusty, sandy, or buggy areas, consider replacing it every six months. Of course, you can inspect its condition at any time. Most air filters are easy to replace.

Install the Air Filter

Modern air filters are round or rectangular. You can purchase replacement filters at auto parts stores and many large discount stores. Make sure that the filter you install is the correct one for the model car *and the engine*. To replace an air filter, follow the steps below:

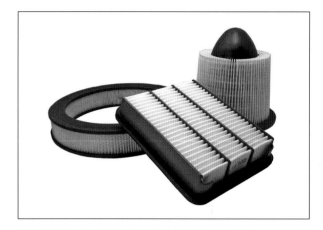

1 Identify the air intake tube in the engine compartment and follow it to the engine. In the path, there is an air cleaner assembly or housing.

2 Open the air cleaner housing. Some units have clips on the side that must be released. Others have screws.

3 Remove the air filter. Most simply lift out of the housing.

4 Install the new air filter in the same position as the old one.

5 Close and fasten the air cleaner housing.

FAQ

How can I tell if the filter element I'm buying is of good quality?

Open the box and inspect it. Even better, open the boxes of a few filters of various prices. You can visually compare the products to determine which is of better quality materials. If the difference in price is only a few dollars, go with the better-quality filter. Also, put a label on the filter when you install it, indicating the date.

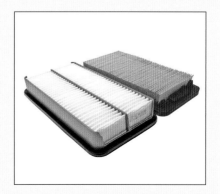

Inspect the Exhaust System

Your car's exhaust system has an important job: to efficiently get rid of gases produced by the engine's internal combustion. To perform this task, the exhaust system has many parts. Fortunately, there are no moving parts that can wear out. Heat and corrosion are its enemies. You probably won't replace any of these parts yourself, but inspecting the system every three months can help you spot conditions before they become problems.

Exhaust System Components

Components of a typical automotive exhaust system include:

- **Exhaust manifold:** draws exhaust gases from the engine's combustion chambers.
- **Catalytic converter:** converts unburned hydrocarbons into water vapor, carbon dioxide, and other less harmful gases.
- **Muffler:** reduces the noise made by engine exhaust.
- **Resonator:** reduces additional noise made by engine exhaust.
- **EGR valve:** recirculates some exhaust gas into the engine's air/fuel mixture.
- **Exhaust pipes:** distribute gases from the manifold to the catalytic converter, muffler, and resonator, and then to the rear of the vehicle.
- **Clamps, brackets, and hangers:** support the components under the car while protecting it from exhaust heat.

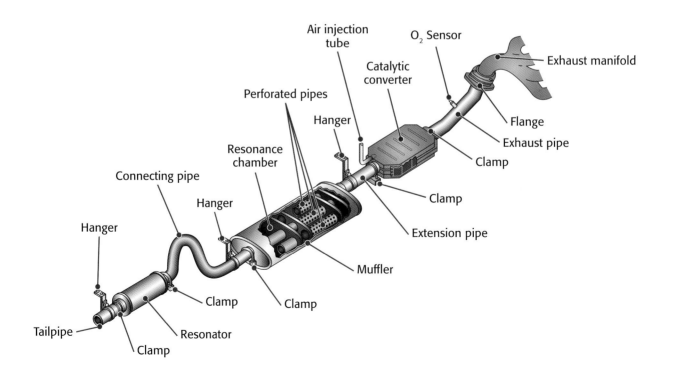

Check the Exhaust System

Here's how to visually check your car's exhaust system for potential problems:

1 Make sure that the engine and exhaust are cool.

2 Inspect the exhaust system as follows:

- **Exhaust manifold:** Look for leaks, gasket damage, rust, holes, and loose or broken bolts.

- **Catalytic converter:** Look for bluish or brownish discoloration (caused by overheating), rust, corrosion, and road damage.

- **Muffler/resonator:** Look for holes, road damage, and rust.

- **Exhaust pipes:** Look for holes, rust, and dents.

- **Clamps, brackets, hangers, and heat shields:** Look for damage, rust, missing parts, and loose bolts.

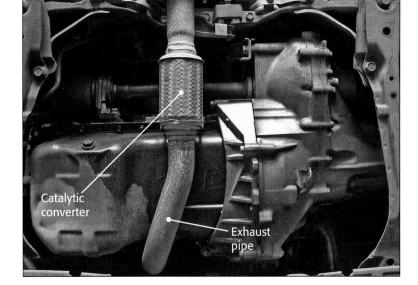

Catalytic converter

Exhaust pipe

TIP

The exhaust gas recirculation (EGR) system includes a valve or electronic controls to introduce exhaust gases into the engine to reduce emissions. If troubleshooting or your OBD-II reader finds fault with the EGR valve, install an exact replacement unit, available at auto parts stores. Refer to your car's service manual for location, specific instructions, and cautions.

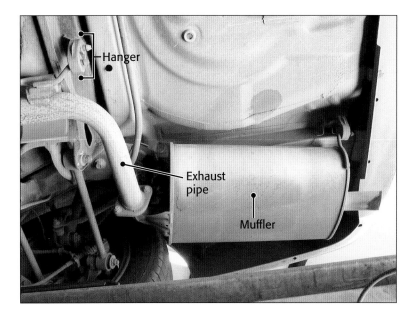

Hanger

Exhaust pipe

Muffler

chapter 7

Suspension and Steering

Your car—and its passengers and cargo—rides on the suspension system. Modern cars have suspension systems designed for many thousands of miles of trouble-free riding. It's a good thing, too, because working on automotive suspension can require specialized tools. Even so, you can be a smart car owner by knowing how the suspension and related steering systems work and identifying conditions before they become problems. This chapter describes both the suspension and the steering system for better understanding and care.

How the Suspension and Steering Systems Work

Everyone wants a smooth ride with no bumps, agile steering, and road-gripping tires. Together, the suspension and steering systems make this possible.

Components of the Suspension and Steering Systems

Understanding how the various components work in the suspension and steering systems can help you troubleshoot problems and better inspect these components for potential issues.

Steering

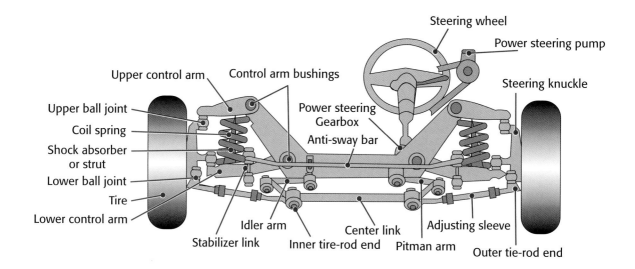

Suspension

SUSPENSION

The function of your car's suspension system is to keep the occupants comfortable as the car travels over uneven surfaces. Components of a typical suspension system include:

- Springs (coil, leaf, torsion-bar)
- Shock absorbers and struts
- Upper and lower control arms

STEERING

The steering system transfers the movement of the steering wheel to the two front wheels. Components of a typical steering system include:

- Steering wheel
- Steering gear (manual or power)
- Power steering unit
- Steering linkage (pitman arm, center link, idler arm, tie rods, sockets)

SHOCK ABSORBERS AND STRUTS

Shock absorbers and struts reduce the bounce that suspension springs develop as the car drives over uneven surfaces. You can inspect the condition of your car's shock absorbers and struts (see page 115). If you feel comfortable working on your car, then you can also replace them yourself.

Note: *There are two kinds of struts: the MacPherson and the Chapman, each named after its designer. The MacPherson strut is the more common of the two.*

MacPherson strut

Shock absorber

FAQ

Can I perform any of these steering system fixes myself?
Have at it! If you're so inclined, you can do it yourself. You will need the car's service manual for specifics, and most of the specialized tools are readily available. Make sure you safely jack up and block the car's front end.

CONTINUED ON NEXT PAGE

TIRES

Tires have evolved quickly to keep up with other advances in automotive technology. Though they look similar to tires of previous decades, today's tires are much safer and sturdier and have a longer life. You can minimize tire wear by rotating them periodically. You can also select quality tires, though installing tires on wheels requires advanced tools and should be left to a tire shop or mechanic.

Bias tires are strengthened by crisscross plies. *Bias-belted tires* add two or more belts for added strength. *Belted radial tires* run the plies radially, and then add two or more belts for even more strength. Newer designs add steel-reinforced sidewalls to the tires.

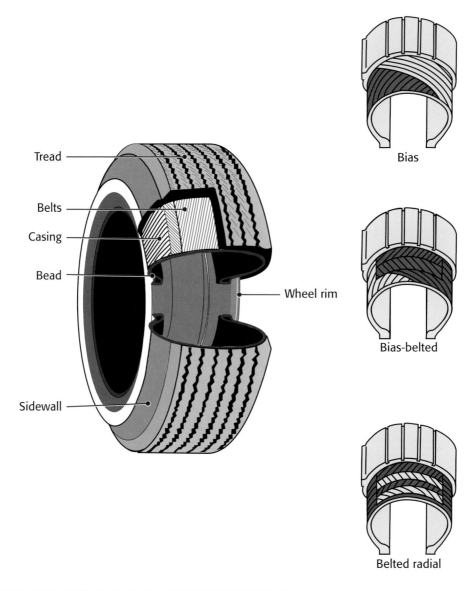

Tread

Belts

Casing

Bead

Sidewall

Wheel rim

Bias

Bias-belted

Belted radial

Steering problems include excessive movement in the steering wheel, feeling road bumps through the steering wheel, hard steering, pulling to one side, and drifting. The causes include worn steering gear, leaking hoses, and worn components in the steering linkage. Most car owners don't fix these problems themselves, but you can learn to identify them and keep the mechanic honest.

Diagnosing Steering Issues

STEERING PLAY

Steering play occurs when the steering wheel moves before the front wheels turn. Some play is normal. However, excessive play can mean the following:

- The steering linkage or tie-rod ends are worn or damaged.
- The steering gear is worn or damaged.
- The steering gear mounting bolts are loose.

FEEDBACK

Feedback is feeling imperfections in the road surface in the steering wheel. Feedback can mean the following:

- The steering linkage or tie-rod ends are worn or damaged.
- The steering gear mounting bolts are loose.
- The suspension bushings or ball joints are loose.

HARD STEERING

Hard steering occurs when the steering wheel is difficult to turn, especially near its turning limits. Hard steering can mean the following:

- The steering gear needs adjustment.
- The manual steering gear is low on lubricant.
- The power steering fluid is low. Check hoses for leaks.
- The power steering pump is faulty and needs to be replaced.

PULLING AND DRIFTING

As you drive, your car may *pull* or *drift* to one side, requiring you to pull the steering wheel in the opposite direction to make the car go straight. Pulling and drifting can mean the following:

- The wheel alignment is incorrect.
- The steering linkage or tie-rod ends are worn or damaged.
- The tires are not balanced or have other load problems.
- The vehicle, especially a pickup, is carrying an unbalanced load.
- If the pulling and drifting occurs when braking, the brakes may need service.

Inspect the Steering Alignment

For fast and smooth steering, your car's steering and suspension systems must be aligned. Car owners don't have the tools and equipment to resolve alignment problems, but you can know how it all works.

Wheel Alignment 101

Alignment angles are designed into the car for optimum steering. These angles should be checked once a year or when tires are replaced.

- *Caster* is the vertical tilt of a front wheel. Zero caster means that there is no tilt; positive caster tilts toward the rear of the car, and negative caster toward the front.

- *Camber* is the tilt of the top of a front wheel in or out. Positive is out and negative is in.

- *Toe* is the position of the front edge of both front tires relative to each other. If the front edges are closer than the rear edges, they are toe in. If the front edges are farther from each other than the rear edges, they are toe out.

There are other alignment specifications, depending on the car's design. Alignment is accomplished by adjusting or replacing steering system components. Computerized wheel alignment machines calculate the various angles and are used by technicians to make the proper adjustments.

Caster

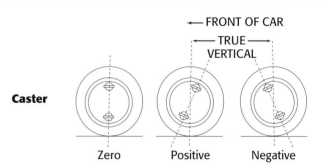

Zero   Positive   Negative

Camber

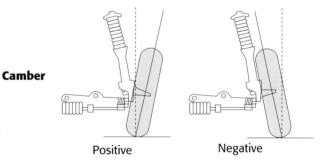

Positive   Negative

Toe

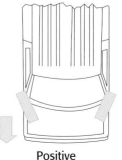

Positive (Toe in)   Negative (Toe out)

TIP

Not only can poor alignment cause steering problems, but it can also wear out tires faster and cause dangerous stress on steering components. In addition to normal wear, alignment problems can be caused by the front wheels hitting a curb, stone, or pothole.

Shock absorbers and struts dampen the movement of the suspension springs. If you hit a bump and the springs' reaction continues, the shocks or struts may need to be replaced. You probably don't have the tools and equipment to replace them, but you can be a smarter consumer and hire people who do.

Shock Absorbers 101

Most modern cars have *coil springs* in the front suspension and *leaf (flat) springs* in the rear. Shock absorbers and struts are connected to the car's frame so that the action of the springs after a bump is dampened.

A *shock absorber* (a) is designed to dampen the movement of a car spring. It does so with hydraulic fluid and/or air pressure. A *strut* (b) is a similar device that works a little differently, but includes a shock absorber within it.

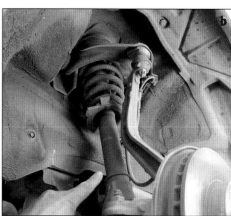

FAQ

What should I inspect on a shock absorber?

Two things: check the condition of the bushings and check for leaks. *Bushings* are the rubber connections at the top and bottom of shocks. Make sure that they are securely fastened and that the rubber gasket is not worn out. Also inspect the tube for exterior leaks of hydraulic fluid.

Rotate Tires

To equalize tire wear, many car and tire manufacturers recommend that tires be rotated periodically. The rotation pattern depends on the type of car (front-, rear-, or four-wheel drive), the tire design, and how the car is driven.

Tire Rotation 101

You can rotate the tires yourself if you have sufficient jacks and stands to safely lift the entire car. However, most consumers have the job done at a tire shop or by a mechanic. The process is similar to changing a flat tire (refer to Chapter 12) except that you are taking a tire off one wheel and moving it to another.

Note: *Many tire stores do not charge for rotating tires that they sold.*

Refer to your car's owner's manual for the recommended rotation pattern. Some patterns suggest not mixing front tires with rear tires or not switching from one side to the other. Other patterns include or exclude the spare tire, depending on the type of spare.

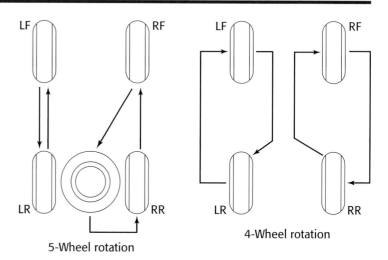

5-Wheel rotation

4-Wheel rotation

How often should tires be rotated? Manufacturers often suggest rotating radials every 7,500 miles and bias and bias-belted tires every 6,000 miles. This means that each tire will be on each wheel once during its typical lifetime. Longer-wear tires may be rotated every 10,000 miles, as the manufacturer suggests.

FAQ

What about snow tires?

If you want to seasonally replace rear road tires with snow tires, follow this rotation:

1. Remove and store the front tires.
2. Move the rear tires to the front.
3. Install the snow tires on the rear.

Don't rotate studded snow tires.

Tires are designed to provide traction. Depending on the tread design, the tires may be more effective in rain, mud, snow, off-road, speed, commuting, or other conditions. Knowing how to buy tires will make you a smarter car owner.

Buying Tires

When buying replacement tires, first consider the car manufacturer's recommendation. Check the placard on one of the doorjambs. It indicates the size and design of the tire, as well as recommended or maximum tire pressure. You don't *have* to buy replacement tires of the same specifications, but you should stay close to them for safety and efficiency. The tire sidewall also includes useful information.

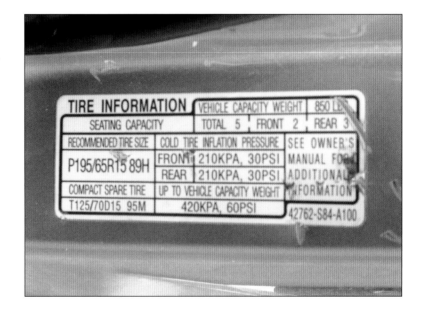

- Size (for example, P195/75R14 = Passenger car, 195mm wide, 75 height-to-width ratio, Radial, for a 14-inch rim)

- Maximum load rating (the maximum weight the tire can carry at the recommended tire pressure)

- Tread wear (100/soft to 500/hard)

- Traction rating (A/more, B/average, C/less)

- Temperature rating (A/higher, B/average, C/lower)

- Date code (week and year; for example, 4208 = 42nd week of 2008)

- Safety warnings

TIP

The tire's date code is important because tire materials age with time. For example, a tire that is six or more years old with no use or wear may not be safe. When buying "new" tires, make sure that the manufacture date is recent.

Date code

8

Brakes

If you can't stop, you have a problem. Before the problem arises, take some time to learn about brake care and maintenance. You can do the work yourself or hire someone to do it for you. In either case, you need to know how your car stops, how it goes, and how to tell when your brakes have problems. This chapter takes you inside your car's brake system.

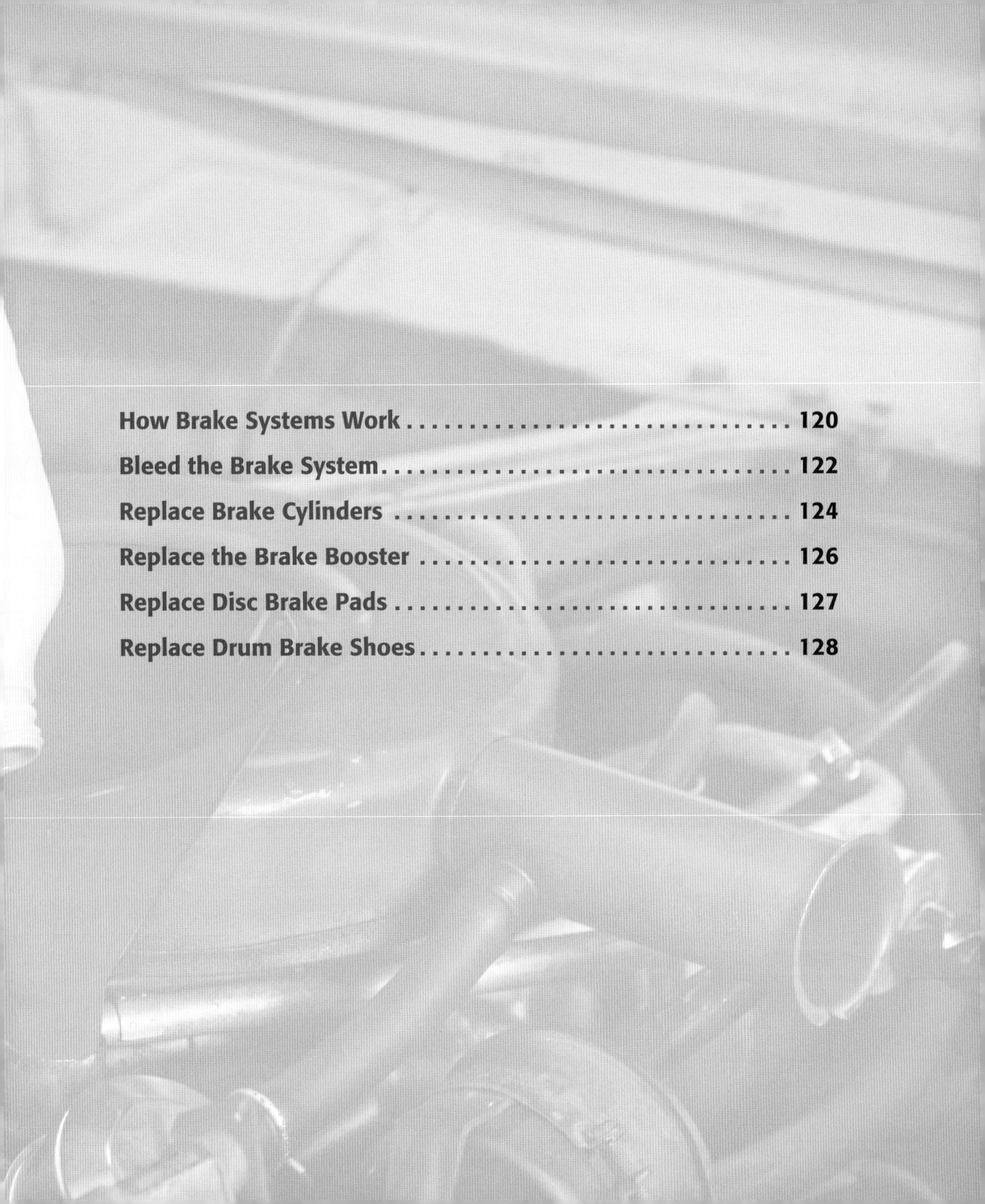

How Brake Systems Work

Now that you have your car running smoothly, how do you stop it? By taking good care of the brake system. Taking care of the brake system means understanding how each component of the brake system works.

Understand Brake System Components

The primary components of modern car brake systems are the master cylinder, brake booster, brake lines, disc brake assembly, and drum brake assembly. An antilock brake system (ABS) assists with control. You'll learn how brake components work, the potential problems, and how to fix them.

Brake System

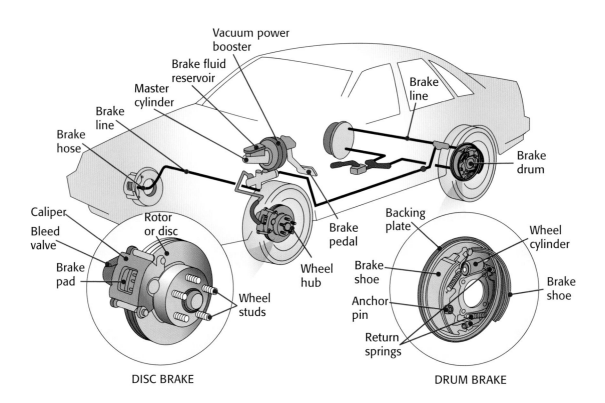

DISC BRAKE

DRUM BRAKE

MASTER CYLINDER

Brake systems use hydraulic fluid that magnifies pressure on the brake pedal to the brakes at the four wheels. The fluid comes from the master cylinder. You learned how to check master cylinder brake fluid in Chapter 3 (see page 36).

BRAKE BOOSTER

To further magnify the brake pedal pressure, a vacuum- or hydraulic-operated booster is attached to the master cylinder. If the booster fails, your brakes still work, but the pedal is very difficult to press. An experienced do-it-yourselfer can replace a brake booster.

DISC BRAKES

The brakes on the front wheels of most modern cars are disc brakes. Some cars have disc brakes on all four wheels. Disc brakes stop the car by forcing brake pads against, or pinching, a rotating disc. The friction causes heat, and the components are cooled by the surrounding air. Brakes can stop your car for many thousands of miles before they need attention or replacement.

DRUM BRAKES

Rear brakes typically account for only about one-third of the total braking for a car. Drum brakes are an older, but still effective, brake design used on the rear wheels of many modern cars. Drum brakes stop the car by forcing brake shoes against the inside of a rotating drum. Vents in the brake assembly enable air to cool the hot components.

FAQ

What is an ABS?

Modern cars have an antilock brake system (ABS) that minimizes skidding when you hit the brakes hard. It proportionately adjusts brake fluid to the four wheels as needed for a smooth stop. The ABS system also works with your car's powertrain control module (PCM), discussed in Chapter 6.

Bleed the Brake System

The master brake cylinder stores and controls brake fluid and connects to wheel cylinders at each wheel through brake lines. Air can enter the system if the master cylinder fluid level is below the minimum level due to a loose connection or a hole in a line. You'll know that you have air in your lines if your brake pedal pressure feels soft. After you repair the cause, you may need to remove air from the brake system by "bleeding" the brakes.

Preparation

To manually bleed brake lines of air, you need a helper. Mechanics use pressure-bleeding equipment that replaces the helper.

Before you begin, have a container of fresh brake fluid on hand. Never reuse old hydraulic fluid. As noted in Chapter 3, most modern cars use DOT-3 brake fluid. Check your car's owner's manual for specific requirements.

In addition, you need a clear bleeder hose and a glass or plastic jar to collect excess brake fluid. Brake bleeding kits are available at auto parts stores.

You also need to safely access the rear side of all four wheels, one at a time. If you cannot access easily, you may need to jack up the car to reach the brake bleeder screws.

Note: *Refer to your car's service manual for specific instructions.*

FAQ

How can I avoid getting air in the brake system?

Make sure that the master cylinder has sufficient brake fluid (refer to Chapter 3) and does not draw air into the system. Also, visually inspect the brake lines at least once a year, looking for fluid leaks, loose fittings, and damaged lines. If you replace the brake lines, you have to bleed the brakes.

Bleed the Brakes

The purpose of bleeding a brake system is to force out any air in the master cylinder, brake lines, and wheel cylinders. To do so, you open up each of the wheel cylinders as your helper presses on the brake pedal. Once air is forced out at one wheel cylinder, you close the bleeder screw and move on to the next wheel.

Note: Make sure that the brake fluid level in the master cylinder is always above the ADD line during this process. Otherwise, you will be adding more air to the system.

To bleed a brake system, follow these steps:

1 Attach the bleeder hose to the bleeder screw.

2 Place the glass jar in position to catch excess brake fluid. The jar must be located below the level of the master cylinder.

3 Ask your helper to pump the brake pedal a few times and then hold it down with moderate pressure.

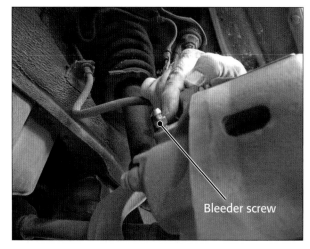

Bleeder screw

4 Slowly open the bleeder valve and allow the fluid/air mixture to flow to the glass jar.

5 Close the bleeder valve.

6 Ask your helper to slowly release the brake pedal.

7 Repeat the process as needed (typically three to five times), until no air bubbles are in the bleeder hose.

8 Refill the master cylinder with *new brake fluid* and perform the same procedure on the other brakes.

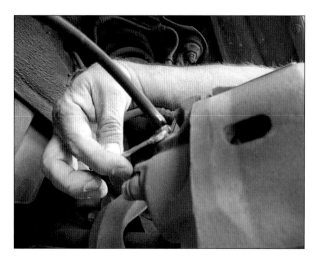

Replace Brake Cylinders

Brake cylinders are located at each of the four wheels. Like all other automotive components, brake cylinders can fail. Rather than repair them, most mechanics simply replace them with new or rebuilt units. You can, too.

When the brake pedal is depressed, a rod pushes on a piston in the master cylinder, which, in turn, forces hydraulic fluid through the brake lines and to the wheel cylinders. The pressure then forces the brake pads or shoes against the discs or drums to stop the car by friction.

Replace Wheel Cylinders

Defective wheel cylinders often reveal themselves by leaking fluid or by obvious damage. In addition, mechanics and consumers may opt to replace wheel cylinders—even if they aren't leaking—if they are replacing other parts in the brake system. To replace wheel cylinders, follow these steps:

1 Locate the wheel cylinder. On disc brake wheels, they typically are on the back side of the brake plate. On drum brake wheels, they are between the two brake shoes.

2 Follow the car's service manual for disassembly instructions. You may need to remove other components to access the wheel cylinders.

3 Remove the wheel cylinder and replace it with an exact replacement, available at auto parts stores.

4 Bleed air from the brake system (see the previous page) as needed.

Note: *On disc brakes, it is often more efficient to replace the entire disc caliper than to replace just the wheel cylinder.*

TIP

Brake fluid contains polyglycols and polyglycol ethers, both toxic chemicals. Avoid contact with your eyes, and wash your hands thoroughly after handling brake fluid. Brake fluid can also damage automotive paint; if dripped or spilled, immediately wash the area with water and an absorbent cloth.

Replace the Master Cylinder

Your car's master cylinder is located either in the engine compartment or under the car and attached to the frame. Refer to the service manual for the location and specific instructions for removal and replacement. In general, to replace a master brake cylinder, you do the following:

Note: Refer to your car's service manual for specific safety requirements for working on pressurized brake systems.

1 Disconnect the negative battery cable for electrical safety.

2 Disconnect the electrical connectors from the master cylinder.

3 Remove the master cylinder reservoir cap.

4 Remove brake fluid from the master cylinder using a siphon. Alternately, a clean turkey baster works.

5 Disconnect the fluid lines from the master cylinder.

6 Unfasten the mounting nuts that attach the master cylinder to the brake booster.

7 Remove the master cylinder from the brake booster.

8 Install the new or rebuilt replacement master cylinder in the reverse order.

9 Bleed the master cylinder of air as recommended by the manufacturer.

Replace the Brake Booster

Your car's brake system probably has a brake booster to further magnify pedal pressure and stop the car more easily. If the brake pressure you need to apply to stop your car changes all of a sudden, then the booster may be the problem. Refer to the service manual for troubleshooting tips. If the booster is the culprit, you can replace it yourself, or at least be better informed when you hire a mechanic to do so (see FAQ below).

Replace a Vacuum or Hydraulic Brake Booster

On many cars, the booster uses a vacuum; on other cars, it uses hydraulics. Vacuum brake boosters use the vacuum developed by the engine to magnify the force of the brake pedal to the master cylinder. Hydraulic brake boosters use hydraulic fluid, typically shared with the power steering unit, to magnify the brake pedal force to power the master cylinder.

To replace a vacuum or hydraulic brake booster, follow these steps:

1 Remove the master brake booster (see "Replace the Master Cylinder" on the previous page).

2 Disconnect the vacuum hoses from the brake booster.

3 Inside the passenger compartment, disconnect the brake pedal from the booster shaft.

4 Remove the bolts that attach the booster to the engine compartment's rear wall (firewall).

5 Remove the booster from the engine compartment.

6 Install the new or rebuilt brake booster in the reverse order.

7 Install the old, or a new or rebuilt, master cylinder (see "Replace the Master Cylinder" on the previous page).

8 Bleed the master cylinder of air as recommended by the manufacturer.

FAQ

Is this really a job I can do myself?

Maybe. If you have a full set of socket wrenches and have done other intermediate-level car repairs, you can replace a brake booster and perform other brake maintenance and repairs. Be aware that if you run into a problem, you won't be able to drive the car to your favorite mechanic; you'll have to call a tow truck. If you're comfortable with this, then have at it!

Disc brakes operate like those on many bicycles. Pressure on the brake controller forces pads against rotating wheels. On cars, the brake pad, held in place by the caliper, presses against the spinning rotor.

How will you know if you need to replace components in your car's disc brake system? Many brake pads have wear sensors that you can either hear or see. Yes, that scraping noise you hear from your wheels may be the wear sensors. Other cars have a light on the dashboard that illuminates when pads are worn.

If the dashboard light or your ears tell you that the disc brakes need servicing, plan to get it done within the next 100 miles of driving. Waiting too long allows the worn brake pad to damage the disc rotor, which can not only be unsafe, but will add to the cost of the brake repair.

Install Disc Brake Pads

The most common disc brake parts to wear, by design, are the brake pads. To replace brake pads, follow these steps:

1 Remove brake fluid from the master cylinder by using a siphon. Alternately, a clean turkey baster works.

2 Safely jack up the corner or the entire car, and place jack stands under it.

3 Remove the wheel and tire.

4 Inspect the brake assembly, looking for signs of fluid leaks, broken brake lines, or a damaged brake rotor. If necessary, repair these problems before continuing.

5 Lift and remove the caliper assembly from the rotor. To keep the caliper housing out of the way, some housings rotate on a pivot. Other housings must be hung in place using a wire attached to the car frame.

6 Remove the brake pads from the caliper assembly.

7 If needed, install a C-clamp over the caliper and tighten the clamp to force the piston into the bore.

8 Install new pads into the calipers.

9 Place the caliper with new pads over the rotor and insert the installation bolts.

10 Tighten the bolts.

11 Move to the next brake and repeat. When you are finished, bleed the brake system (see page 123), and then reinstall the wheels and tires.

Replace Drum Brake Shoes

Drum brakes operate by pushing brake shoes against the inside of the spinning drum that's attached to the wheel and tire. The resulting friction slows the car down.

Like disc brakes, many drum brake shoes have audible or visual wear indicators. In addition, you can inspect them and compare the shoe surface thickness to the manufacturer's recommendation, typically .08 inch.

Don't wait too long to get your brakes serviced. If your brakes need servicing and you let it go, you allow the worn brake shoe to damage the brake drum, which can be both unsafe as well as an additional cost to your brake repair. So once you hear that the drum brakes need servicing (or once the dashboard light tells you so), plan to get it done within the next 100 miles of driving.

Install Drum Brake Shoes

The most common drum brake parts to wear, by design, are the brake shoes. To replace brake shoes, follow these steps:

1. Remove the brake fluid from the master cylinder by using a siphon. Alternately, a clean turkey baster works.

2. Safely jack up the corner or the entire car, and place jack stands under it.

3. Remove the wheel and tire.

4. Remove the brake drum. Most manufacturers suggest that you use a hub or wheel puller (available at auto parts stores).

5. Inspect the brake drum lining for cracking, glazing, contamination, and wear. If necessary, take damaged brake drums to a machine shop for repair, or replace the drums.

6. Clamp the two brake shoes to the backing plate to relieve pressure on the shoe springs.

7. Remove the brake shoe springs and adjuster.

8. Remove the brake shoes.

9. Install new brake shoes as recommended by the manufacturer. The shorter (primary) brake shoe is installed closer to the front of the car; the longer (secondary) shoe is closer to the rear.

10 Reinstall the brake shoe springs and adjuster. If in doubt about assembly, refer to the car's service manual or the other drum brake.

11 Install the brake drum.

12 Adjust the brakes until you hear a slight drag between the drum and shoes.

13 Move to the next brake and repeat. When you are finished, bleed the brake system (see page 123), and then reinstall the wheels and tires.

FAQ

Do drum brakes need to be adjusted?

Modern brakes are self-adjusting. A mechanism inside the brake assembly automatically compensates for wear by moving the shoes so they are as close to the drum as possible without dragging on it. However, if the adjuster is installed incorrectly, it can actually make stopping more difficult with wear.

9

Engine

Thus far in this book, you've learned how to check and maintain a variety of systems on your car. The most important system—and the most difficult to maintain—is the engine. The engine powers your car. For it to do so, you or your mechanic must make sure that it has sufficient compression and that the timing and drive belts are doing their jobs. The engine also powers the alternator, the power steering unit, and the optional air conditioner. This chapter shows you how to care for these vital components.

There's a lot going on in your car's engine. You've suspected as much. But exactly how does the car's engine work to control all those explosions without blowing itself apart? This section tells you how each major component of the engine works together to power your car.

Engine Components

Major parts of your car's engine include the cylinder block and the cylinder head. Each houses numerous other parts. Belts interconnect them and other components.

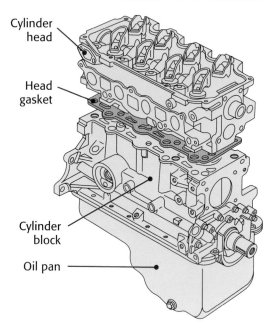

Cylinder head

Head gasket

Cylinder block

Oil pan

CYLINDER BLOCK

The engine cylinder block is the lowest and largest part of your engine. In it are the piston, the crankshaft, and the connecting rods that connect them.

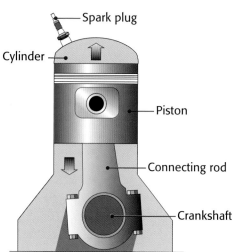

Spark plug

Cylinder

Piston

Connecting rod

Crankshaft

CYLINDER HEAD

The cylinder head sits atop the cylinder block and has valves, a camshaft, the intake manifold that feeds fuel and air to the engine, and the exhaust manifold that takes the exhaust gases from the engine. There are both intake and exhaust valves inside the cylinder head. In addition, V-engines (such as V-6 and V-8) typically have two heads, one for each group of cylinders.

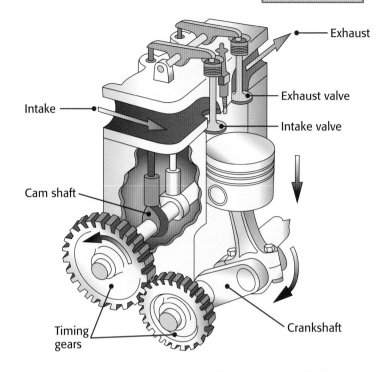

Exhaust

Exhaust valve

Intake valve

Intake

Cam shaft

Timing gears

Crankshaft

TIMING BELT

To synchronize the efforts in the block with those in the head(s), cars have a timing belt or timing chain. It makes sure that the valves in the head open exactly when the piston in the block needs them to.

In addition, the engine uses drive belts to power other devices. These devices include the alternator, power steering unit, radiator fan, and optional air conditioner.

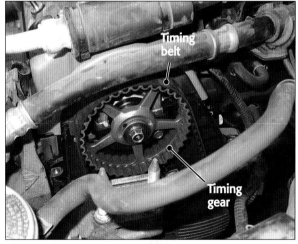

Timing belt

Timing gear

FAQ

Can I really work on my engine?

Once you're familiar with the components and have performed other parts replacement jobs, you should be ready to tackle engine work—on *some* cars. Refer to the car's service manual for specific instructions. Some cars are designed for easier consumer repairs than others. If the instructions look doable, consider these intermediate jobs.

Engines require that the fuel/air mixture introduced into the individual cylinders be compressed to a specific pressure. That's one of the jobs of the pistons. However, if the cylinder leaks even a little, the compression may be lower than needed for efficient operation. If troubleshooting tells you that cylinder compression may be low, you can test compression yourself or hire a mechanic to do it.

Compression Test 101

A compression test can indicate whether cylinders are developing sufficient compression (a cutaway photo of a cylinder is shown at right). Your car's service manual can help you better interpret the test results so that you can either perform the needed repair or talk more knowledgeably with your mechanic. Test cylinder compression whenever you are replacing spark plugs (refer to Chapter 5) or when the car begins using more oil.

To perform a compression test on engine cylinders, you need a special tool called a *compression gauge* or tester. These are available for purchase at auto parts stores, or for rent through larger rental centers.

Compression gauges display pressure as pounds per square inch (psi) and metric kilopascals (kPa). Your car's service manual has the manufacturer's recommended compression levels for the engine. Use a compression gauge that screws into the cylinder's spark plug hole.

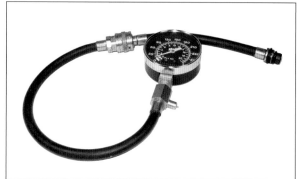

Steps for Testing Compression

Following are typical steps for testing engine cylinder compression:

1 Disable the ignition system and fuel injection system, following your car's service manual instructions.

2 Prop the throttle plate into a fully open position.

3 Remove *all* of the engine's spark plugs (refer to Chapter 5).

4 Connect a remote starter button to the starter system (refer to Chapter 5).

5 Install the compression gauge into the first cylinder's spark plug hole.

6 Press the remote starter button until the engine makes *one* full revolution, and then stop. Read the gauge and write down the results.

7 Press the remote starter button again for a few seconds, until the gauge meter reading does not increase. Write down the results.

8 Press the pressure release valve on the gauge.

9 Continue the test on all the other cylinders. If the test begins to drain the battery, connect a battery charger before continuing.

10 If compression in a cylinder is low, squirt a small amount of engine oil into the cylinder and repeat the test (called a *wet test*). If compression is now higher, the piston rings have a poor seal. Refer to the service manual or see a mechanic for further work.

TIP

Engine Numbers

Just as cars have a VIN (refer to Chapter 2), engines have a unique EIN, or engine identification number. It's located on or near the valve cover. In addition, the block has an identification number. You need these numbers when searching for replacement parts for your engine.

Replace the Timing Belt

Replacing an engine timing belt can be done by consumers on many cars, but most owners hire a mechanic instead. The easier ones to replace are those that you can see in the engine compartment. Internal timing belts require that covers be removed, which can be a more complex job.

Timing Belt 101

Rotation of the crankshaft is transferred to the camshaft and valves by the timing belt or timing chain. The crankshaft and camshaft(s) have timing marks on them, and the timing belt has grooves or links that assure synchronized action. In addition, all timing belts and most timing chains have an automatic adjuster that does not require service.

Timing belts or chains are either replaced as recommended by the manufacturer, such as every 100,000 miles, or because they break and the car won't go anywhere without one.

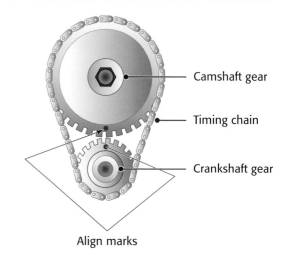

Camshaft gear

Timing chain

Crankshaft gear

Align marks

Install the Timing Belt

Note: *Refer to your car's service manual for specific instructions.*

Following are typical steps for replacing an engine timing belt:

1. Disconnect the negative cable from the battery.
2. Remove the timing cover, if there is one.
3. Align the timing marks on the camshaft sprocket with the mark on the cylinder head. Use chalk or white correction fluid for marks.
4. Remove the crankshaft timing sensor.
5. Loosen the belt tensioner pulley adjustment bolt.
6. Slide the timing belt off the crankshaft sprocket. Make sure that the crankshaft pulley does not rotate.
7. Remove the crankshaft pulley without rotating it.
8. Install the new timing belt around the crankshaft sprocket.
9. Reinstall the crankshaft pulley.

Timing gear

Timing belt

⑩ Verify that the marks on the crankshaft pulley and cylinder head are aligned.

⑪ Reinstall the crankshaft timing sensor.

⑫ Align the timing marks on the camshaft sprocket with the mark on the cylinder head.

⑬ Wrap the timing belt over the camshaft sprocket.

⑭ Make sure that the belt tensioner is applying tension to the timing belt.

⑮ Turn the engine two complete turns (using a socket wrench), and recheck belt tension.

⑯ Turn the engine two additional turns, and verify that the crankshaft and camshaft alignment marks are correct. Adjust as needed.

⑰ Reinstall the timing cover, if there is one, and reconnect the battery.

A *drive belt* is a continuous belt that enables one engine component to drive or power another. Most commonly, drive belts use rotation power from the engine crankshaft to drive the alternator, power steering unit, and air conditioning unit. Losing a drive belt is not as critical as losing a timing belt, but it can soon lead to problems. Changing a drive belt is a relatively easy task once you have some experience with working on your car.

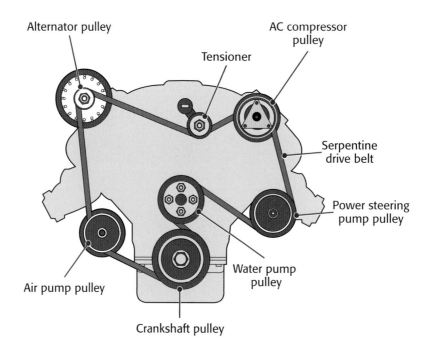

Alternator pulley

AC compressor pulley

Tensioner

Serpentine drive belt

Power steering pump pulley

Water pump pulley

Air pump pulley

Crankshaft pulley

Install a Drive Belt

Refer to Chapter 3 for steps to inspect drive belts.

To replace a drive belt:

1 Trace the path of the drive belt to ensure that you know which belt is to be replaced.

2 Loosen the adjuster with a wrench.

3 Remove the belt from the part pulley.

4 Remove the belt from the engine crankshaft pulley.

5 Inspect the new belt against the old one to verify that it is of the same width, depth, length, and design.

6 Install the new drive belt over each of the pulleys. Your car's service manual may recommend a specific order.

7 Move the adjuster as needed to apply recommended tension to the belt and tighten the adjuster. Some drive belts have automatic tensioners.

> **Note:** *Touch the outside of the belt midway between two pulleys, and push on it to measure how far it moves. Most manufacturers recommend that a belt deflect about ½ inch. Alternately, use a tension tester, available at auto parts stores.*

8 Start the engine and visually inspect the drive belt for proper operation.

Adjuster

Pulley   Drive belt

TIP

Travel Tip

If you're planning a vacation, consider buying a backup drive belt and putting it—with some basic tools—in the trunk of your car. You probably won't need it, but if you do, you may save the price of a tow, expensive parts, and a greedy mechanic. Consider buying backup radiator hoses as well, especially if you plan a trip through a hot climate. Of course, for safety, you can install new drive belts and radiator hoses *before* you head out on that trip.

An automotive air conditioner (AC) operates similarly to a home AC. ACs cool air by pulling heat out of it. The evaporator draws the air out of the passenger compartment, the condenser gets rid of the heat, and the compressor moves the air. The resulting air is cooler.

The biggest problem with ACs is a lack of cool air. Although you can't do much work on AC systems, you can perform regular checks and service to keep the cool air flowing longer.

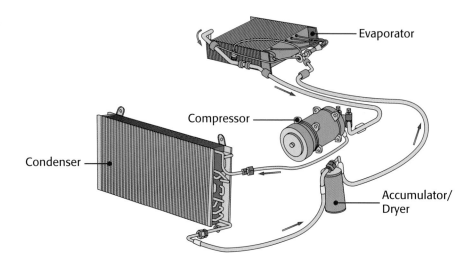

Evaporator

Compressor

Condenser

Accumulator/
Dryer

AC Inspection

① Check the AC compressor belt on the engine for condition and tension. Make sure that bolts holding the compressor in place are tight.

② Check the condition of lines and hoses between the evaporator and condenser for condition. If hoses are damaged, you may need to replace them and recharge the system.

TIP

AC Recharge Kits
You can purchase R-134A automotive air conditioner recharge kits at auto parts stores. Some kits also include a leak sealer that can fix small leaks in the system. Ask the auto parts store clerk for assistance in selecting an appropriate AC recharge or sealant kit for your car.

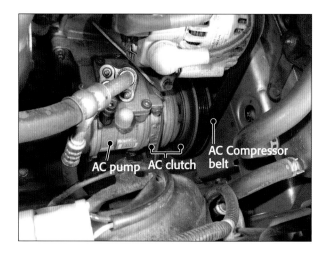

AC pump   AC clutch   AC Compressor belt

❸ Clean dead bugs, leaves, and other debris from the surface of the condenser using a soft brush and water.

❹ Start the engine and turn the air conditioner on high, then low, and then high again. Listen for the AC compressor to click on and off, indicating that the compressor clutch is working correctly. If it does not click on and off, it may require service.

❺ For R12 systems, check the refrigerant sight glass located on or near the receiver/dryer (check the car's service manual). Run the AC for about five minutes, and then look in the sight glass on top. If you see what looks like clear water flowing through the sight glass, the refrigerant level is okay.

FAQ

Is the refrigerant in my older car's AC the correct type?

Good question! Cars built before about 1996 use Refrigerant 12 (R-12 or Freon), which is now unavailable for environmental reasons. Its replacement is R-134A (SUVA), a less-effective but more environmentally friendly refrigerant. If your old R-12 system needs more refrigerant, you must have it serviced by an authorized AC service center that will evacuate all R-12 from the system and recharge it with R-134A.

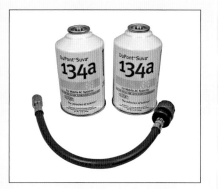

chapter 10

Body

No matter what the fuel efficiency is, many people buy cars based primarily on the body style and condition. Fortunately, maintaining a car's body condition is relatively easy. This chapter shows you how to keep your car looking fresh and new long after it rolls 100,000, 200,000, or more miles.

Auto Body Basics

Ever since cars were first manufactured more than a century ago, the auto frame has been built and the body mounted on top of it. Pickups and other trucks are still built that way. However, most modern cars are built with a unitized body design, called *unibody*, that integrates the body and frame. More plastics are used in the bodies, and paints have evolved, making today's car bodies easier to care for.

Breaking Down the Auto Body

Bodies are more than just metal, plastic, and paint. They come in different shapes and sizes, include several components, and are created with new design methods and materials that make them more fuel efficient.

BODY COMPONENTS

Automotive bodies include:

- **Hood:** The hinged lid covering the engine (on front-engine cars).
- **Fenders:** Body panels mounted over and around the wheels.
- **Doors:** Hinged panels for access to the passenger compartment.
- **Roof:** The panel covering the top of the passenger compartment.
- **Trunk:** The hinged lid covering the rear storage area. Called a *hatch* on cars with storage areas that are integrated into the passenger compartment.
- **Windows:** Viewing openings covered in safety glass.

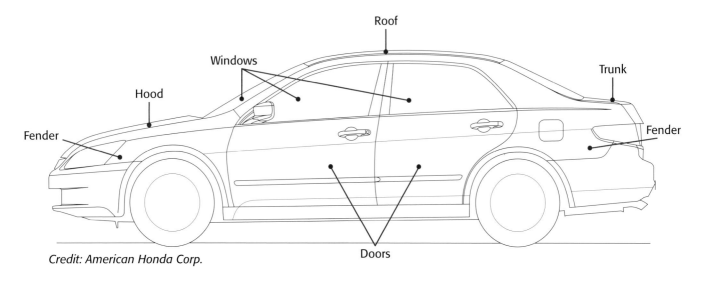

Credit: American Honda Corp.

BODY MATERIALS

Cars are getting lighter due to new design methods and materials. The average sedan today weighs 3,000 pounds, compared to 4,500 pounds three decades ago. Most are built primarily of steel and plastics. Engines are now made of aluminum rather than heavier iron. Lighter weight means better fuel efficiency.

Modern painting techniques make it difficult to determine whether a body panel is made of steel or plastic until you touch it. However, because both steel and plastic components include a clear-coat finish, maintenance is essentially the same.

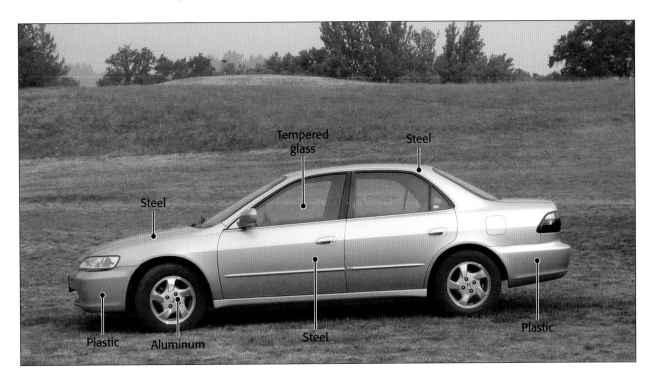

FAQ

What is a body panel?

A *body panel* is a removable component of a car's body. Body panels include the front fenders, rear fenders (called *quarter panels*), bumpers, hood, trunk, roof, and doors. If the panel has multiple layers (like a door), the outside layer is called the *skin*.

Washing and Waxing

Modern cars are painted with a primer, a color paint, and then a clear coat that protects the color paint from fading or chipping as old, two-stage paint jobs did. To care for your car's body, wash it at least once a month and wax it every six months. Wash and wax more frequently if it sits under trees or in dusty areas. Hand-washing and -waxing keeps the finish in good condition longer. Drive-through car washes can be tough on finishes and should be used sparingly.

Wash a Car

To wash a car:

1 Gather washing materials. Use car wash products rather than dishwashing or laundry detergent that can damage car finishes.

2 Find a shady spot where direct sun won't dry the surface too quickly.

Note: If available, use warm rather than cold water to wash and rinse your car.

3 Thoroughly soak the car with water to remove loose dirt and contaminants.

4 Starting with the top of the car and working down, wash all surfaces with car wash and a wash mitt or big sponge. Don't allow the soap to dry on the surface; if necessary, wash the car in sections.

5 Rinse the car with a soft spray.

6 Starting with the top of the car, dry the surfaces with clean, absorbent towels (preferably cotton) or a chamois skin. If there is standing water, you can remove some of it with a clean squeegee.

7 Admire your clean car.

Note: Some car manufacturers recommend that you do not use drive-through car washes, as the brushes can dull the clear-coat finish.

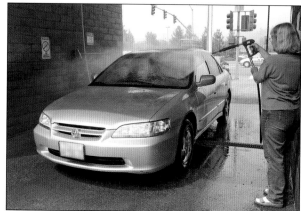

Wax a Car

You can protect a car's clear coat by periodically applying car wax.

1 Wash and dry your car thoroughly (see previous page).

2 Apply polish and/or wax following the manufacturer's instructions.

3 Allow the product to dry, typically just a few minutes.

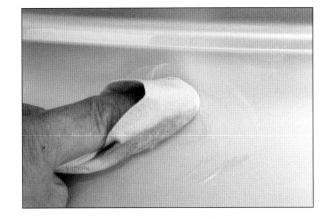

4 Wipe away the product and buff it out with a soft cloth or electric buffer made for auto detailing.

5 If there is product residue, carefully rinse and dry the surface.

FAQ

What's the difference between a car wax and a car polish?

A wax protects the finish. A polish cleans *and* protects the finish. Polishes remove oxidized finish, bugs, tar, and other contaminants. Many polishes are polish/wax products. For tough spots, you may need a cleaner or a rubbing compound to remove sap or dry bugs. Refer to the product's label and directions for specific applications and instructions.

Engine Cleaning

An engine compartment is a dirty place that houses oils and other fluids, as well as a lot of heat. It can quickly get dirty. Once a year, take a look at your car's engine compartment to see if it would benefit from the efforts of a thorough cleaning.

Plan the Job

If you're planning to clean your car's engine compartment, don't do it at home where contaminants can wash into the sewer system or stain the driveway. Instead, take it to a nearby do-it-yourself car wash that is set up for engine cleaning. You may need to take the following materials with you:

- Engine cleaner
- Plastic bags or plastic wrap
- Rubber bands
- Stiff brush
- Shop towels or old rags

TIP

Commercial Car Washes

If you do use a commercial car wash, select one that is close to your home. You don't want to spray cold water on a hot aluminum engine, as it can cause damage. If you must drive far, make an intermittent stop (such as for lunch) near the car wash so the engine will be warm, but not hot when you clean it.

TIP

Visual Inspection

As you're looking around the engine compartment, search for potential leaks, especially around the oil filler cap. A leak may indicate a problem that you can solve with a new cap or by tightening fasteners.

Clean the Engine

Before starting the cleaning process, prepare the engine compartment for the water and cleaning chemicals.

1. Disconnect the negative cable from the battery. If your car radio has a security code, make sure you know it so that you can reset it after you reconnect the battery.

2. Cover the air intake (near the front of the engine compartment, in front of the air filter) using a plastic bag or plastic wrap. Also cover any electronics that may be damaged by the water, such as the distributor or ignition wires. Make sure that the oil and transmission dipsticks are covered so that water doesn't leak down the tubes.

3. Use a stiff brush to remove excess oils, grease, and dirt from the engine compartment.

4. Apply the engine cleaner as directed by the manufacturer. Alternately, you can use a mixture of liquid dish detergent and water.

5. Use the car wash setting for engine cleaning to thoroughly clean the engine compartment. If you are doing the job at home, use the hardest stream setting on a water hose sprayer or a power washer on the lowest pressure setting.

6. Remove the plastic bags or wrap from the protected components.

7. Use shop towels or old rags to dry the components, especially the electronics.

8. Start the engine to continue drying the car with engine heat. Some ignition systems may not run smoothly until the wires dry.

Interior Cleaning

You will spend countless hours in the interior of your car. It may be like a second home. If so, make sure it's fresh and clean to make driving your car more enjoyable.

Cleaning Different Surfaces

CLEAN UPHOLSTERY

What's that stain? In most cars, it could be grease, soda, special sauce, a dog stain, or something else. Here's how you can clean it from the upholstery:

1. Identify the type of upholstery: vinyl, leather, cloth, or plastic.

   Note: Some "leather" upholsteries are only real leather where the driver and passengers make contact (seat, steering wheel) and simulated-leather vinyl everywhere else.

2. Identify the stain: grease, chemical, ink, bio-matter, and so on.

3. Use a clean brush or rag to begin cleaning the stain. Carefully brush away solids without spreading the stain. Blot liquids. You can use a vacuum if assured that it won't spread the stain.

4. Select the appropriate upholstery cleaning product, available at auto parts stores. Read the product directions to determine which product best removes the type of stain from the kind of upholstery fabric you have.

5. If the selected upholstery cleaner doesn't work, consider household cleaners. Test each one first at an inconspicuous location to make sure that it doesn't damage the upholstery fabric.

6. Allow the cleaned upholstery to air-dry.

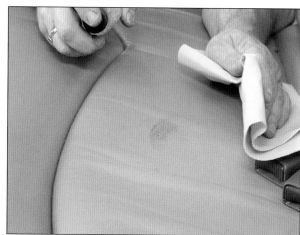

CLEAN GLASS

Glass takes up a lot of surface on your car. A car wash cleans exterior glass, but interior glass needs cleaning, too—especially if you carry smokers, children, pets, or other live cargo.

Household glass cleaners are adequate for cleaning vehicle windows. However, automotive glass cleaners are made to clean bugs and films that household window cleaners may not. In addition, automotive glass cleaners typically don't include ammonia, which can be acrid in an enclosed car.

To clean automotive glass:

1 Choose a shady area so that the sun doesn't dry the cleaner too quickly.

2 Spray the cleaner, beginning at the top of the window and working your way down so that the spray runs down the glass to thinly cover the surface. Be careful not to overspray to other surfaces.

3 Wipe off the cleaner with clean paper towels or lint-free towels. Don't use dirty cleaning materials.

CLEAN OTHER SURFACES

Auto parts stores and other retail outlets sell a variety of car interior surface cleaners, primarily for vinyl parts. Follow the product instructions, testing it in an inconspicuous location first. Note that some offer a glossy shine while others leave a matte or dull shine. Shiny is pretty—until the sun hits it and the glare creates a driving hazard.

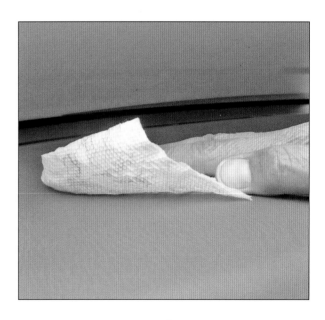

TIP

Caution

Many cars have a wire grid embossed onto the inside of the rear window. When activated, this electric grid warms up and defrosts the glass. Be careful not to damage the grid when cleaning. Clean the window by carefully wiping it horizontally, following the grid path.

Eliminate an Odor

Odors in enclosed cars can quickly become overpowering. Here's how you can find the cause of an odor and eliminate it.

Find the Cause

A temporary odor in your car will be gone before you determine the cause. A lingering odor can be distracting to the driver and passengers. The first step is to find what may be causing the odor.

1 Open up the car doors, turn on the ventilation fan, and let the odor escape if it can. If it doesn't, continue.

2 Identify the type of odor: musty, putrid, sweet, and so on.

3 Identify the general location of the odor. Is it strongest in the front seat area, rear seat, trunk, engine compartment, or under the vehicle?

4 Search deeper. Check under the seats, below the floor mats, in the glove box, in the heater vent, below the trunk floor, near the engine, and so on.

5 Remove the cause. If it is liquid, use rags and cleaners to dry and clean the area. If a stain, see "Interior Cleaning" on page 150. If it is biological, remove the cause and clean the surface.

Clear the Odor

Numerous short-term products mask an odor with a fragrance. However, the preferred method of removing an odor is to find and eliminate the cause and then clean the surfaces and clear the air.

1. If you removed the cause of the odor from inside the passenger compartment, open all the windows and doors and turn on all the ventilation fans. Allow the interior to air out for at least 20 minutes before verifying that the odor is clear.

2. If the odor emanated from the engine compartment, clean up the source, making sure to clean any spillage as well. A hot engine can renew traces of the odor source.

3. If the source of the odor was in the car's trunk, open the trunk and remove any fabric or materials that may have absorbed the odor. If needed, place a fan in the compartment to clear out trapped odors.

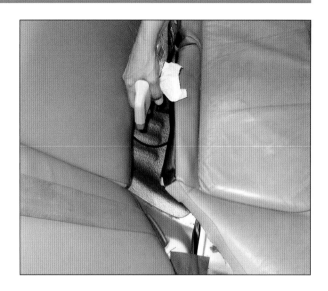

TIP

Common Car Odors

Many things can cause a lingering odor in a car. Most common is trapped moisture, such as water or other liquids that age in a hidden location. A child can "save" food under a seat or a floor mat. Body fluid stains can intensify with age. A rodent can become trapped and die in the trunk, in a heater duct, or under a seat. Fluids leaking on a hot engine can be odoriferous.

Rust isn't as prevalent on modern cars as it was on older ones. Today's cars have less steel and more rust inhibitors, and are designed for better water drainage. Even so, rust spots can begin on nearly any car and attempt to consume it like a cancer. Your job is to find rust and stop it.

Identify and Get Rid of Rust

RUST 101

Rust is a brittle, red-brown coating, technically known as *hydrated ferric oxide*. It forms when oxygen (as in the air), iron (as in steel), and water (as in rain) combine. Paint and other finishes can protect steel from water and air, but once the finish is damaged, rust can begin.

Surface rust is easy to identify and remove. If it is only on the surface of the metal and hasn't eaten away any metal, then thoroughly clean it and replace the sealing finish, and the rust probably won't return. Imbedded rust that goes deeper or through the metal is more difficult to remove. First, you must replace the metal that was consumed, then add a sealing finish to keep the rust from returning.

FAQ

Should I worry about car rust?

That depends on where you live. If you're in an arid climate, your car may never rust. If you're in a snowy climate where caustic road salts are used, your used car may already have spots of it. Sea salt also accelerates the formation of rust on cars (and metal boats). The best plan is to inspect your car at each washing and proactively treat the rust.

TREAT RUST

Treating rust before it becomes a problem is a relatively easy job. Treating it later can be expensive.

1 Search for rust conditions. Look on the steel components of the car body for chips, nicks, and spots where rust can start or has started. Dark spots under the paint can mean that rust is coming through the metal from the other side.

2 Treat the situation. Brush or scrape the rust away to the bare metal. Treat the surface with a rust inhibitor, available at auto parts stores. Prime and repaint as needed. Touch-up primers and paints also are available at auto parts stores. Follow the manufacturer's directions.

PREVENT RUST

If you live in a salty climate or one where caustic road salts are used on snowy and icy roads, your car will benefit from undercoating. Though you can apply rust-inhibiting undercoating under your car just like paint, professional undercoating services do a more thorough job. Undercoating products are available under various brand names as well as through auto dealers and detailers.

TIP

Look Underneath

Rust isn't dumb enough to show up only where you can see it. Rust prefers places where you can't easily find and eradicate it. As you inspect your car for rust, look carefully under the car, especially in places where salts can sit for months without being disturbed.

Remove Scratches and Dents

Your car is susceptible to "parking lot rash." Symptoms are dings and dents that appear on vehicles after being parked at shopping malls, restaurants, and other crowded places. Fortunately, you can remove many dents and scratches with a little effort and some know-how.

Remove Scratches

As you learned at the beginning of this chapter, *body panels* are thin metal or plastic components that decoratively cover unibody cars. The finish is relatively thin and can easily be scratched. Fortunately, scratches are simple to remove.

1 Inspect the scratch.

If the scratch is a surface mark, you can probably remove it with rubbing compound (available at auto parts stores) and a soft rag.

If the scratch cuts into the clear-coat layer, you need to clean and touch it up with new clear coat (see "Touch Up Paint" on page 158).

2 Clean or repair the scratch based on what you found.

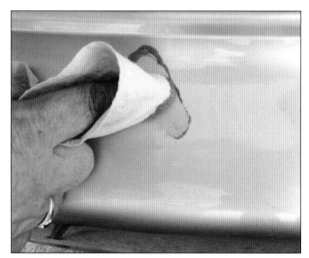

Remove Dents

Small dents in body panels can easily be removed in many cases.

1 Inspect the dent.

If the panel is plastic or thin metal, you may be able to push the dent out from the other side with your hand. Alternately, use a soft rubber mallet, available at auto parts stores.

If the dent does not easily push out by hand, go to Step 2.

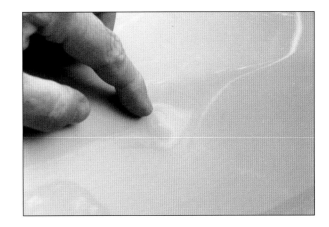

2 Purchase a body suction cup and follow the package directions to pull a small dent out of a body panel. If that doesn't work, go to Step 3.

3 Purchase a dent puller and follow the package directions for larger dents. Most products require that you drill a hole in the center of the dent, insert the tool, and pull the dent toward you.

4 As needed, use a body repair kit, following package directions to smooth out any rough parts of the remaining dent. Repaint the surface as needed (see "Touch Up Paint" on the next page).

5 If necessary, consider replacing the body panel or skin. Most are held in place with clips on the rear side.

2

TIP

Prevent Scratches and Dents
You can prevent many scratches and dents caused by parking lot rash with the following steps:

1. Park away from other cars or take up two spaces in a parking lot.

2. Make sure that the door and bumper trim on your car is firmly in place to deflect shopping carts and other damage. If your car doesn't have bumper trim, you can purchase it at auto parts or auto body stores and install it following the package directions.

Touch Up Paint

You don't have to buy a pressurized paint sprayer to paint small spots on your car. You can purchase pre-mixed touch-up paints and apply them in less time than it takes to set up a sprayer.

Touch-Up 101

Remember that automotive paint is applied in three coats at the factory: primer, color, and protective clear coat. Your touch-up paint job should have the same three coats.

Touch-up paint tools include cap applicators, mixing jar and brushes, and a small, pressurized air gun. Many new cars come with touch-up paint in a jar, with a brush attached to the cap. Artist paintbrushes serve for most automotive touch-up jobs. A hobby air-gun can be an effective body painting tool if you have prior experience. The tools you select depend on the size of the job and your skills.

Paint Small Spots

Before you begin, mask off the area that you will be painting so that extra paint or overspray won't land on nearby surfaces. Use painter's masking tape, which is easier to remove from painted surfaces than other tapes.

To apply touch-up paint on automotive body panels:

1 Remove rust or dents as needed, following the instructions in this chapter.

2 Sand the area to be painted using fine automotive sandpaper or a spot sanding pen. Make sure the surface is even and smooth.

3 Apply the primer following the manufacturer's directions.

4 Apply the color coat following the manufacturer's directions.

5 Apply the clear coat following the manufacturer's directions.

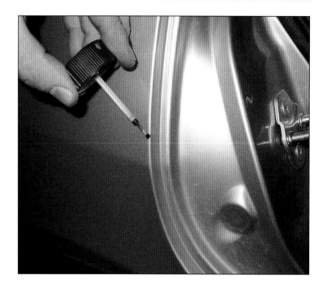

FAQ

How can I make sure that I get an exact paint match?

Car paints are standardized. Auto paint stores know from your car's make and model which paints were used in manufacturing. To confirm, remove the gas cap door from your car (if it is the same color as the body) and take it in when you purchase touch-up paint. You can then test the touch-up paint on the inside and make a visual comparison. Auto paint stores and shops also have equipment that can identify colors by paint samples. If your car is more than a few years old, paint fading may make an exact color match difficult.

Fix a Door

Your car's doors have numerous parts and functions. They include a door latch, lock mechanism, glass, window mechanism, and structural components. Many of these parts can be replaced or adjusted.

Remove Door Panel

The first task of inspecting, adjusting, or replacing door components is to gain access. Doors on most modern vehicles have hidden screws and clips that hold the panel onto the door frame. Tools needed include a cross-head (Phillips) screwdriver or Allen wrench, a putty knife, and, for roll-up windows, a retainer tool (available at auto parts stores).

Following are general instructions for removing a door panel. Refer to your car's service manual for specific instructions on your make and model.

1 Open the car door.

2 Remove the door lock button on the top edge of the door by lifting and unscrewing it.

3 Remove the door handle that opens the door from the inside. Attachment screws typically are installed behind plastic covers.

4 Remove the window controller:

If your car is equipped with manual windows, remove the handle retainer clip (also called a *circlip*) with a tool made for the job, available at auto parts stores. Alternately, you can carefully use a bent wire to catch the end of the retainer clip and slide it out.

If your car is equipped with power windows, remove the controller by removing the covered screws or carefully prying the unit out of the door with a putty knife or other thin tool. Refer to the car's service manual for specific steps.

5 Check the door for additional attachment screws and remove them.

6 Remove the door panel. Use a putty knife around the door's perimeter to carefully remove the grommets from the holes in the door frame.

7 Carefully remove the plastic weatherproofing sheet covering the door frame. Don't tear it.

Replace Components

Once you have removed the door panel, you can adjust or replace door system components. Make sure that the parts you purchase are exact replacements for your make and model. Power door locks and window switches that aren't working may simply need loose terminals reconnected. Or you may need to replace the locks or switches. Electric switches can be replaced, sometimes without removing the door panel. Refer to your car's service manual for part numbers and specific instructions.

TIP

A door that doesn't close smoothly may only need an adjustment.

1. Open the door.

2. If the latch, located on the door or post, is loose, tighten it with the appropriate screwdriver or wrench.

3. If the hinges, located at the front edge of the door, are loose, tighten them with the appropriate wrench.

Repair Windshield Damage

Nothing is more frustrating than driving down the road only to have a stone chip your windshield. You have two options to get it fixed: hire a professional or do it yourself.

Windshield Repair 101

Road stones can chip your car's windshield before you can avoid them. Fortunately, the glass in modern cars doesn't easily shatter on contact. However, a crack can weaken the glass. A small crack can quickly spread to become a large one that challenges the integrity of the glass. This could take days or years, and you have no way of knowing when it might spread. Not safe! Fortunately, you can repair a small crack yourself with a windshield repair kit, available at auto parts stores.

Before doing your own windshield chip repair, check your auto insurance policy. It may cover the cost of hiring a professional windshield installer or chip repair service to do the job for you.

If your car has a heated windshield, you may want to hire a professional to repair the chip or replace the windshield, as appropriate. Rear windows have wire grids to defrost the surface. Front windshields have a micro-thin metallic coating on the *inside* of the glass. If the outside chip is deeper than the exterior glass, you could damage the interior coating.

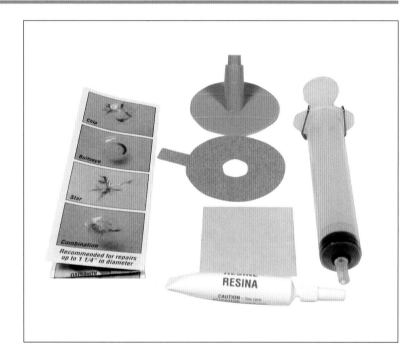

Check your car's owner's manual or service manual for more information. Windshield repair services typically are mobile and can come to your home or office to do the work. If you decide to hire a service, ask your mechanic for recommendations, and ask the service for references first.

Use a Windshield Repair Kit

1. Carefully remove any loose glass from the chip with a toothpick.

2. Clean the windshield with auto glass cleaner. Make sure it is completely dry before continuing.

3. Apply the adhesive disc over the chip.

4. Place the plastic pedestal or dam on top of the disc, following the instructions on the kit container.

5. Insert the applicator on the pedestal and push on the plunger to force filler into the chipped area. Stop when the dam is full.

6. Allow the plastic to harden as directed by the kit manufacturer.

7. Remove the applicator, pedestal, and disc.

chapter 11

Easy Maintenance Guide

Maintaining your car is easy and rewarding. You can extend the life of your car by many thousands of miles—and reduce the cost of driving—by performing a few easy tasks illustrated in this book. This chapter summarizes those tasks in a simple system of easy car maintenance. Have fun!

Be Prepared

Many drivers put off regular maintenance because it isn't convenient. You have a free Saturday morning, but not enough time to buy the needed parts *and* do the maintenance job. Or you don't have the proper tools. So plan ahead.

Preparation

To prepare for regular car maintenance, follow these steps:

1. Schedule maintenance jobs in advance. Mark them on your calendar and list the parts and tools you'll need. Next time you're near an auto parts store, pick up the parts and tools and have them ready.

2. Review the process before you start. Make sure you know what you'll be doing, that you have what's needed, and that you are prepared.

3. Dress for the job. Don't ruin good clothing with grease or battery acid. If you prefer, keep a shop coat or pair of mechanic's overalls for working on your car.

4. Work safely. Don't be in a hurry. Make sure you have the necessary safety equipment.

FAQ

How often should I do maintenance work on my car?

As recommended by the manufacturer. Many automakers suggest that if most of your trips are farther than 10 miles, typically at highway speeds, and you don't tow anything, then you can perform regular service at 7,500-mile intervals. Otherwise, cut the interval in half: about every 3,500 to 4,000 miles. Use an auto log or notebook to track maintenance.

Chapter 1 shows you how to open the car's hood and suggests things to inspect when you fill up your car's fuel tank(s). Chapter 3 adds specific instructions. Here's a summary.

Inspections to Perform at the Gas Station

- ❏ Check the oil level. Use a window cleaning towel or shop towel to check the level of oil on the engine dipstick. Keep an extra container of recommended oil in the trunk.

- ❏ Check the tire pressure. Use a tire pressure gauge to check the pressure in all four tires and the spare. If you don't have time to check them all, check any tires that look less inflated than the others.

- ❏ Check the washer fluid level. Make sure the reservoir has sufficient washer fluid or water to clean the windshield in case of dust, salt, or bugs.

- ❏ Visually inspect the battery, belts, hoses, wiper blades, and other components for potential problems. Replace as needed.

- ❏ If you have an OBD-II diagnostics tool, run a quick test. Record the results in your auto log or notebook for reference when you get home and can look up the codes.

Air and Water
Many gas stations (no longer called service stations because there is no service involved) offer air for tires and water for radiators. If your car needs these services, look around the perimeter of the station for air and water equipment. Some stations charge for these.

Every 3 Months or 3,500 Miles

Assuming that you're an average car owner, you drive 12,000 to 15,000 miles a year. If these are easy highway miles, you may opt to skip the oil/filter change suggested in this section. However, you still need to do the other quarterly services to keep your car in top condition.

Quarterly Service

Note: If this recommendation of quarterly service contradicts what your car owner's manual says, follow the manual.

- ❑ Complete the tasks under "When You Fill Up" (page 167).

- ❑ Check the brake fluid level (refer to Chapter 3).

- ❑ Check the transmission fluid level (refer to Chapter 3).

- ❑ Check the power steering fluid level (refer to Chapter 3).

- ❑ Change the oil and oil filter (refer to Chapter 4). Before you skip this step, remember that the cost of parts is typically less than $20—much less than the cost of problems that bad oil can cause.

- ❑ Check or replace the air filter (refer to Chapter 6).

FAQ

How can I remember to perform quarterly service?
If you expect to drive 3,000 miles or more in the next three months, the easiest way to remember service is to post a mileage service note where you will see it when you get in the car. If you don't expect that many miles, mark your calendar three months after the last service.

Twice a year—depending on how and where you drive—you should set aside some quality time with your car. You'll need some tools and a workspace. If you choose not to perform the work yourself, visit a trusted mechanic.

Semiannual Service

❑ Complete the tasks under "When You Fill Up" (page 167) and quarterly service tasks (see the previous page).

❑ Check the drive belts and coolant hoses (refer to Chapter 3).

❑ Check the power steering fluid level (refer to Chapter 3).

❑ Check the brake fluid level (refer to Chapter 3).

❑ Rotate tires as recommended (refer to Chapter 7).

❑ Check the brake pads and shoes (refer to Chapter 8).

Find a Mechanic

One of the advantages of preventive car maintenance is that you will have fewer road emergencies where you have little choice of who the mechanic is. At home, you can choose the best available mechanic, based on personal recommendations, your own experience, and the suggestions in Chapter 1. You can partner with your mechanic toward keeping your car safely and cost-effectively on the road.

After your car has been driven 12,000 to 15,000 miles—or 12 months have passed—it's ready for another service session. Fortunately, there are only a couple of added tasks.

Annual Service

- ❏ Complete the tasks under "When You Fill Up" (page 167), as well as the quarterly and semi-annual service tasks on the previous two pages.
- ❏ Replace the wiper blades (refer to Chapter 3).
- ❏ Inspect the shock absorbers and struts (refer to Chapter 7).

TIP

Cheap Insurance

There are two schools of thought regarding car maintenance. You can wait until something fails to replace it, or you can replace it before it fails, even though it may have some service left in it. Because car components typically don't fail where tools and a workspace are handy, failure may mean being towed to an unknown service shop and being at the mercy of the service manager. Pinching pennies can be expensive.

Modern cars don't require service as often as older models, yet they last longer. For example, cars of a half-century ago required oil changes every 1,000 to 3,000 miles and were expected to last less than 100,000 miles. In modern cars, 100,000 miles is middle age. Biannual service about every 30,000 miles can keep cars from aging prematurely.

Biannual Service

- ❏ Complete the tasks under "When You Fill Up" (page 167), as well as the quarterly, semiannual, and annual service tasks described on the previous pages.
- ❏ Replace the coolant (refer to Chapter 4).
- ❏ Service the transmission (refer to Chapter 4).

FAQ

How long can I keep my car running?

With regular maintenance, a modern car is designed to operate 100,000 miles or more without major problems. Many well-cared-for cars reach 200,000 miles. A few cars on the road are still rolling with more than 500,000 miles on the odometer.

Every 3 Years or 45,000 Miles

A car with 45,000 miles on the odometer is still young with plenty of miles ahead—if it is properly maintained. The average car on the road is more than seven years old. You can keep your car off the side of the road with regular service.

Triannual Service

- ❏ Complete the tasks under "When You Fill Up" (page 167), as well as the quarterly, semi-annual, and annual service tasks described in the previous pages.
- ❏ Replace the radiator and heater hoses (refer to Chapter 4).
- ❏ Replace the battery (refer to Chapter 5).
- ❏ Replace the drive belts (refer to Chapter 9).

TIP

Your Mileage May Vary

In maintaining your car, remember that service intervals are recommended, not legislated. As you learn how to interpret your car's signs, you may decide to extend intervals or make them more frequent during harsh seasons or severe service conditions. You're in the driver's seat.

What would a vacation be without a car? Whether you are going to the airport or traveling cross-country, you want to make sure that you arrive on time with minimal problems. That means making sure that your car is ready *before* the trip begins. Use Chapter 3 as your guide.

Pre-trip Service

❏ Make sure that the scheduled service tasks outlined in this chapter are up-to-date.

❏ Check the oil level.

❏ Check the coolant level.

❏ Check the radiator and heater hoses.

❏ Check the drive belts.

❏ Check the headlights, brake lights, and other lamps.

❏ Check the tire pressure and inspect the tires for damage or excessive wear.

❏ Check that the spare tire and jack are ready.

❏ If you have a road service policy, check that you have the contact information and policy number.

❏ Take this book with you—just in case!

Road Emergencies

If you're regularly performing the preventive maintenance tasks discussed in Chapter 3, you may not face road emergencies. However, a prior owner or another driver of the car may not have been as diligent, and now you're stuck at the side of the road. Or you've been involved in an accident. This chapter offers clear instructions to get yourself back home safely with proven ideas for handling common road emergencies, such as an accident, a breakdown, a flat tire, overheating, your car not starting, and locking yourself out.

Prepare for Emergencies

Most road emergencies are avoidable. Good maintenance can help. Even so, you should prepare yourself and your car for potential emergencies that can be annoying or possibly dangerous.

How much preparation you need for driving depends on when and where you drive. You need only basic tools and road flares for an emergency during a commute. A winter trip emergency requires more planning.

Basic Emergency Supplies

Make sure to keep a toolbox in your car for emergencies. In addition to your insurance card and basic tools (see Chapter 2), consider adding the following items, available at auto parts stores:

- Emergency road flares or lights
- Flashlight with spare batteries
- Jumper cables (to start a car from another car's battery)
- Spare fuses
- Paper towels or clean rags
- Air pump (mechanical or 12v)
- Small shovel
- Emergency road service phone number
- Change for a pay telephone
- Radiator hose repair tape or duct tape

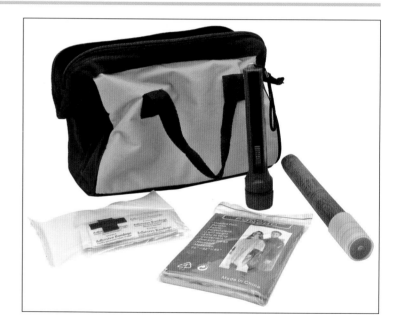

WINTER EMERGENCIES

In some climates, a winter breakdown can be life-threatening. In addition to the basic emergency supplies listed on the previous page, harsh winter driving should include the following:

- Windshield scraper and brush for snow
- Warm clothing
- Nonperishable snacks
- Drinking water (keep inside the passenger compartment)
- Warm blanket (keep inside the passenger compartment)
- Engine heater (required for winter driving in colder climates)
- Traction aids (see Tip below)

Also remember that your car may need a higher concentration of coolant/ antifreeze in the radiator during the coldest months. You can buy a hydrometer or test strips at an auto parts store to test the antifreeze's protection range.

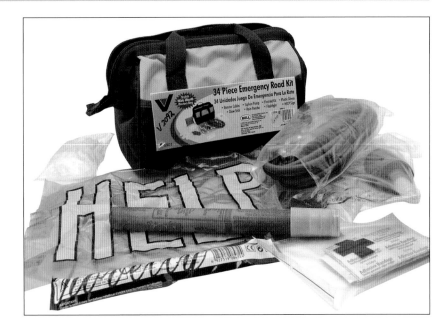

SUMMER EMERGENCIES

You can be ready for hot-weather car emergencies with the following items:

- Extra coolant or water for the car
- Water or a sports drink for the passengers
- Light hats and cotton clothing

TIP

Driving on roads with snow, ice, or mud is more difficult and requires additional emergency aids to help your car's tires get traction if it gets stuck. Recommended traction aids include tire chains, sand, gravel, cat litter, and three-tab asphalt roofing shingles (easy to store in the trunk).

Report an Accident

Nearly all drivers are involved in an accident over their driving years. Hopefully, they are minor, and no one is injured. In any case, you should know what to do if you are involved in a car accident.

At the Scene

When an accident occurs, you must remain at the scene until you have identified any damage and conferred with the other car or property owner and/or the police. Following are things you can do to keep the incident from getting worse:

1. Be calm. If you are not calm, find a passenger or passerby who can help you assess the situation and be a witness.

2. Make sure that all passengers are safely moved off the road as practical. An accident can soon cause another, and people standing in the road can be injured.

   Note: Some state laws require that damaged vehicles be removed from the road immediately if possible.

3. Check yourself and others for injuries.

4. If there are injuries, contact local emergency services by calling 911.

5. If there are no injuries, report the accident if the property damage is probably above your insurance deductible or if the other driver insists.

6. If the other driver is calm, exchange insurance information. Otherwise, write down the car's license number and description and wait for the police to arrive.

   Note: In some situations, the other driver may not be insured or the car may not have the correct license plate. You may need uninsured motorist coverage for damage and possible injuries.

7. Determine whether your car is safe to drive or requires a tow vehicle. Police can assist you in making arrangements and in cleaning up any road debris.

At Home

Hopefully, you already know your state's requirements for reporting accidents that involve a motor vehicle. If not, find out now, before you need to know. Some states require that property damage over a specific amount be reported. Local law enforcement also may direct you as to whether you need to report an accident. In addition, your auto insurance company can offer advice and even checklists to guide you in case of an accident. Do the following when you arrive home after an accident:

1 Be calm. The accident may cause a delayed emotional reaction, and you may become agitated once you get home.

2 Gather all information about the accident.

3 Call your insurance company's accident reporting phone number, typically found on your insurance card.

Note: *Some insurance companies prefer that you call them from the accident scene so they can discuss the incident with the police and get a report number directly.*

4 Move on with your life. Don't become angry or obsessed with the incident. If you or others are injured, continue care and be supportive. Thousands of car accidents occur every day. By being prepared and calm, you can endure it.

TIP

Police, judges, and insurance adjustors will determine who was at fault. In the meantime, *do not admit fault or liability.* Nor should you blame passengers or other drivers. Instead, wait for the police and discuss the event only with the police and your insurance adjustor.

Manage a Breakdown

Even with preventive maintenance, cars can break down: liquid leaks from underneath or a new noise sounds like a serious problem. Knowing what to look for can help you determine whether the leak or noise indicates a serious problem that needs repair or replacement.

Fluid Leaks

Sometimes it's tricky to figure out whether a spot of liquid under the car should be a concern. What should you do if you see a potential leak?

1. Look under the car to determine whether anything is dripping. If not, move the car and look again. The problem may be that you had parked on top of another car's leak.

2. Identify the general location of the leak. Is it just below the engine, transmission, differential, or radiator, or behind a wheel? Remember that the liquid may not fall directly below where it is leaking.

3. Identify the liquid. In general, oil is black, automatic transmission fluid is red, radiator coolant is green or yellow, and water (commonly condensation from the air conditioner) is clear.

4. Find the source of the leak and stop it.

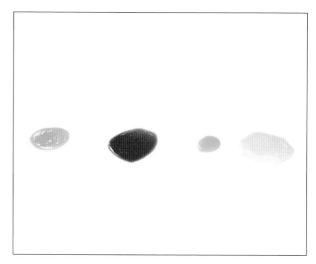

Unusual Sounds

As you drive your car, you will get to know how it sounds. New or unusual sounds can warn you of impending problems, or the noise can just be an open window and a nearby diesel truck. So what should you listen for? The following list indicates the source of many common car problem sounds and where to get more information.

- Squealing in the engine compartment can be caused by loose or worn drive belts (see Chapters 3 and 9).

- A loud hum near the engine can be caused by a faulty alternator or water pump (refer to Chapter 5).

- A rhythmic thud from the engine can be caused by an engine bearing wearing out—a serious problem! See your mechanic.

- A rapid pinging noise from the engine can be caused by low-grade gasoline (refer to Chapter 1).

- A whine from the automatic transmission can be caused by a hydraulic pump going out (refer to Chapter 3).

- Squeaking brakes can be caused by worn brake pads or shoes (see Chapter 8).

- Vibration when you apply the brakes can be caused by unevenly worn brake components. If the steering wheel shakes, the cause may be worn front brakes. If the car seat shakes, the problem may be worn rear brakes (see Chapter 8).

- Clunks when you drive over rougher roads can be caused by worn-out suspension parts (see Chapter 7).

TIP

Many highways have motorist aid call boxes installed at regular intervals. They serve as emergency telephones that are answered by a state or local police dispatcher. Most call boxes are numbered to help the motorist identify his or her location. Call boxes in rural areas often are powered by photovoltaic (solar) cells. Some are built to be wheelchair accessible and have equipment for the hearing impaired. Some even offer language translation services.

You can use call boxes to request police, fire, or towing services. Most are not set up to make other telephone calls. In addition, most states do not allow the call boxes to be used for asking directions. Call boxes are installed and funded to help motorists whose vehicles break down.

Change a Flat Tire

The best time to learn about changing a flat tire is before you need to. It is a relatively easy job—just follow the instructions on these two pages.

Jack Up the Car

To remove your car's tire, you must first lift the car higher than its normal position. For this task, you need a jack.

1 Find the tire jack. Most cars have tire jacks located at one side of the trunk interior. Other locations include under the trunk's false floor (where the spare tire may also be). Some vehicles have jacks in a corner of the engine compartment.

2 Place the jack at the car's safe jacking point. A label on the jack or in the trunk, or in the owner's manual, indicates where the jack should be placed for safe operation. On many cars, the jacking point is on the car frame behind a front tire or forward of the rear tire. On other cars, it is directly behind the tire on a jack socket or plate.

Note: To keep the car from rolling, set the emergency brake and place rocks or blocks of wood on both sides of the tire on the same side of the car as the flat tire.

3 Jack up the car until the tire is nearly off the ground, but still touching.

Remove the Tire

To remove the flat tire, follow these steps:

1 As needed, remove the wheel cover by using a pry bar or a large flat screwdriver to get access to the wheel's lug nuts. Set the cover aside.

2 Use a lug wrench to loosen and remove all the lug nuts holding the tire on the car. Place the lug nuts on the wheel cover or together so you can find them later.

3 Jack up the wheel until it no longer touches the ground.

4 Lift off and remove the rim and flat tire.

Install the Spare Tire

Your car's spare tire is in or underneath the trunk. Many modern cars have a compact spare (commonly called a *donut* because of its small size): a high-pressure mini-spare, space-saver spare, or lightweight skin spare. Most are designed only for emergency use to get you to a tire shop or a mechanic. Compact spares typically are limited to speeds of 45 to 50 mph.

To install a spare tire, follow these steps:

1 Place the rim on the wheel lugs.

2 Hand-tighten the lug nuts on the lugs, making sure that the flat side of the lug nut is out.

3 Lower the jack so that the tire touches the ground for support; this stops the wheel from spinning when the lug nuts are tightened.

4 Using the lug wrench, tighten the lug nuts in a crisscross pattern for even tension.

5 Lower the jack and safety stands so the full weight of the car rests on the tire.

6 Put away the jack and remove any wheel blocks before driving.

TIP

Before you go to the effort of changing a tire, determine whether you have road service available to you. If you are a member of an auto club, chances are you have it. Nearly all automotive insurance companies offer an Emergency Road Service option. Check your insurance card. If in doubt, call your insurance agent and ask.

Also consider carrying a spare-tire sealing product, available at auto parts stores. Inserted into the valve stem, the product injects sealant into the tire. Add air to the tire by following the can directions, and it *may* be sealed sufficiently to drive on.

Handle Overheating

Modern car engines are made using aluminum parts that cannot stand up to overheating as well as older engines that were made of iron. An engine that gets too hot can quickly destroy itself. That is why it's vital that you keep your car cool and respond quickly if it isn't.

Respond to an Overheating Car

COOL DOWN

Today's engines operate at high internal temperatures. Your car's cooling system (Chapter 4) must reduce these temperatures so the engine can operate efficiently. Liquid coolant is circulated within the engine, drawing heat out and passing it through the radiator where it is cooled by air.

An engine can overheat if it is low on coolant or is working excessively hard, such as when pulling a heavy load up a hill. Overheating also can occur if the car is moving too slowly to cool the coolant in the radiator. Here's what you can do:

1 Watch your car's engine temperature gauge or light for indications of overheating. Another sign is steam coming from the engine compartment.

2 If the gauge is nearing the red zone, turn off the air conditioner and turn on the heater fan to high to get the coolant flowing. Speed up if possible to get more air through the radiator.

3 If the gauge goes into the red zone (or the light comes on), immediately find a safe place to stop your car. Shut off the engine and *carefully* open the hood so the engine and radiator can cool.

4 Wait at least 20 minutes before inspecting the radiator and hoses for leaks. If you find leaks, determine whether the car can be safely driven to a shop or your garage for repair, or whether it must be towed. If in doubt, call for a tow truck.

Note: If you have Emergency Road Service coverage, contact your insurance provider for assistance.

ADD COOLANT

If the engine has lost coolant through the pressure-regulated radiator cap, do the following:

1 Check the coolant reservoir level (Chapter 3) and fill if indicated. If coolant is not available, use clean water.

2 Wait an additional 20 minutes before attempting to open the radiator cap. Some caps have a lever that can be *carefully* flipped up to relieve pressure in the radiator.

3 Cover the radiator cap with a thick rag or towel to keep the hot coolant from burning your hand.

4 Press down on the cap and twist it counter-clockwise one-quarter turn to relieve some of the pressure without unlocking the cap.

5 Once steam has stopped, cover the cap with a rag and turn the cap until it lifts off the radiator.

Caution: Do not add coolant or water to a hot engine unless it is running. In addition, some car manufacturers suggest that you never add coolant directly to the radiator when the engine is warm, only through the reservoir. Refer to the owner's manual for specifics.

6 Slowly add coolant to the radiator, being careful that escaping steam doesn't spray you.

7 Replace the cap, make sure the coolant reservoir is full, and take your car to a mechanic or your home where the system can be rechecked and repaired as needed.

 FAQ

What causes overheating?
Common causes of engine overheating include the following:

- Damaged radiator hose
- Loose or broken engine drive belt
- Clogged radiator or heater core
- Sticking thermostat
- Clogged engine-block passages

These and other problems are covered in greater detail in Chapter 4.

Make an Unresponsive Car Start

You turn the key, but nothing happens. What's the problem?

In many cases, the problem is a simple one and the solution is just as easy. However, it's still a nuisance. Here are some of the more common causes of a car not starting and what to do about them.

Determine the Problem and Solve It

SEEK OUT SOLUTIONS ON THE DASH

Modern cars have numerous interlocks or steps that all require a signal that everything is working correctly before an engine can start. In many cases, one of these interlocks isn't operating, although sometimes there are even simpler causes. Here's what you can do to find the cause:

1. Check the fuel gauge. The tank may be empty.

2. Remove the key from the ignition and reinsert it; then try again to start it. The ignition switch may not have made full connection.

3. If your car has an automatic transmission, move the gear selector to make sure that it is firmly in the park (P) position. If the car has a manual transmission, does the clutch have to be placed firmly against the floor before it will start? (Many cars require this.)

4. Verify that dash lights go on when the ignition key is in the on position. If they do not, the battery may be dead or a fuse may be blown.

5. Try starting the engine again. Does the starter turn slowly? If so, turn on the car's headlights and try starting again. If the starter turns even more slowly, the battery charge is insufficient to turn the starter. Recharge or replace the battery. Alternately, you can jumpstart your car (see the next page).

Note: If you have Emergency Road Service coverage, contact your insurance provider for assistance.

CHECK UNDER THE HOOD

If you haven't been able to start your car with the previous suggestions, it's time to open the hood and look further:

1 Inspect the battery. Make sure that the cables are firmly connected and that there is no corrosion (Chapter 3).

2 Inspect the alternator. Make sure that the wires are firmly connected. Also make sure that the drive belt is not too loose (Chapter 3).

3 If possible, inspect the starter (usually accessed from under the car). Make sure that the wire from the battery is firmly connected.

Note: If you suspect the starter, tap it a few times with a hammer. This can loosen carbon buildup on the armature brushes and allow it to operate. However, the starter should be replaced.

4 Your car probably needs additional service to start. Have it towed to an auto repair shop or to your home for further service.

JUMPSTART THE CAR

If the previous suggestions haven't helped your car to start, your only option is jumpstarting your car:

1 Make sure the two vehicles are *not* touching each other.

2 Put both cars in PARK (P) or NEUTRAL (N) gear and set the parking brake.

3 Turn off the ignition switch and all accessories on both vehicles.

4 Attach one end of the positive (red) jumper cable to the *disabled* battery's positive (+) terminal.

5 Attach the other end of the positive cable to the *booster* battery's positive terminal.

Caution: Connecting the positive jumper after the negative cable may send a voltage spike to the computer or activate the air bags.

6 Attach one end of the negative (black) jumper cable to the *booster* battery's negative (–) terminal.

7 Attach the other end of the negative cable to an engine ground on the *disabled* vehicle's engine.

8 Attempt to start the disabled vehicle. If necessary, start the jumper vehicle and run the engine at a fast idle.

9 Once the disabled vehicle starts, disconnect the negative cable from the ground, and then the booster battery. Finally, disconnect the positive cable from the booster, and then the other battery.

Deal with the CHECK ENGINE Light

The CHECK ENGINE light on the dashboard of a modern car is both a boon and a bane. It is designed to communicate a potential operating problem to the driver. Which problem? Is it a true or false reading? Will the engine explode or is the gas cap loose?

Maintaining and using your car means that you need to understand and deal with the CHECK ENGINE light.

Behind the Light

The CHECK ENGINE light, also known as the malfunction indicator lamp (MIL), lights up when certain conditions occur. The red or amber light may display CHECK ENGINE, SERVICE ENGINE SOON, CHECK ENGINE SOON, or a similar warning, depending on the car's manufacturer.

Note: *On cars equipped with OBD-II diagnostic reporting systems, a steady MIL indicates a non-critical problem, while a flashing MIL indicates a severe problem.*

Conditions that trigger the MIL vary between manufacturers, models, and years. Some are triggered by sensors in the engine or other primary systems. Older car MILs are triggered by the odometer to remind the driver that service is recommended. In most newer cars, the MIL indicates a problem that may produce excessive pollutant emissions.

If the CHECK ENGINE light comes on, your car's computer may reduce performance until you get it serviced: this is called "limp in" mode.

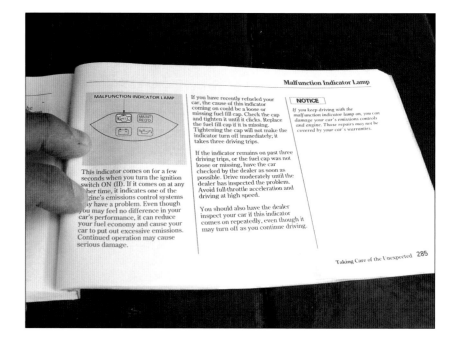

The best advice for understanding your car's MIL is to read the owner's manual. It includes common problems and possible solutions. If it does not, you may need to purchase the manufacturer's repair manual.

Note: *Ethanol and oxygenated gasoline may trigger some MILs that are installed in electronic fuel injected (EFI) cars.*

Digging Deeper

Consider purchasing a hand-held diagnostics tool (Chapter 1) that can read and help you interpret OBD-II codes. These units can report the cause of the MIL indication; software, as well as online or printed instructions, can give you more details and recommend possible solutions.

The diagnostic readers report a diagnostic trouble code (DTC):

- B = body
- C = chassis
- P = power train (engine, transmission, differential)

The code's first number indicates whether the code is standardized among manufacturers (0) or unique to one manufacturer (1). The next three numbers identify the fault. Resources are available, including on the Internet, to help you better understand the codes and find solutions for your specific car.

Note: *Some cars don't require an OBD-II reader to report trouble codes. You can access codes on these cars by turning the ignition to ON and following the manufacturer's steps to display the codes on the digital panel on the dashboard.*

TIP

Don't Deactivate the MIL

No matter how tempting it is to deactivate the MIL, don't do it. Instead, determine the cause and remedy the situation. In most states requiring a smog inspection, having the CHECK ENGINE light (or MIL) on automatically flunks the vehicle. Besides, it may be telling you something you need to know!

Get into Your Locked Car

There are few things more frustrating than looking in the window of your locked car and seeing your keys. Fortunately, there are some things you can do to get inside your car without calling a locksmith. And knowing how to get in can help you keep others out.

Open a Locked Car Door

Depending on your car, unlocking the car door may be relatively easy or very difficult. If it has an activated alarm system, expect to trip the alarm and draw attention to your activities. If it has one of the new anti-theft devices (see next page), it may be impossible to open a locked car door without a key—even if it is yours.

One popular device for unlocking a car door is called a slim-jim, which you can purchase (for emergencies) at larger auto parts stores in states where they are legal. You can make one by cutting and bending a wire coat hanger into a J shape. To open a locked car door with a slim-jim or wire, take the following steps:

1. Identify the location of the door lock button.
2. Identify the location of the interior door handle.
3. Lift the rubber window seal halfway between the door lock button and the interior door handle.
4. Insert the slim-jim or wire into the door cavity to contact the release bar running between the handle and door lock.
5. Lift up on the slim-jim or wire to move the release bar. The door lock button should pop up if successful.
6. Use your keys to start the car.

Note: *If you have Emergency Road Service coverage, contact your insurance provider for assistance. In addition, mall or campus security officers may help you get into a car if you can show proof of ownership.*

Hide a Key

The best way to ensure that you don't lock yourself out is to hide a key on the exterior of your car. Hiding places include the following:

- Behind the license plate, fastened by a license plate screw.

- In a magnetic key box, placed on top of the undercarriage frame or on top of a fuel tank (if metal).

- In a magnetic key box, placed on the underside of a wheel well.

- Anywhere under the car where you can tape it in place and it won't fall off.

TIP

Anti-theft Devices

As you can see, many cars are relatively easy to unlock with simple tools and techniques. Technology tries to stay ahead of thieves. Here are some of the latest anti-theft systems for cars.

- Newer car locks are more difficult to pick, and the keys are more difficult to duplicate.

- Many modern cars have a master key that opens any lock, and a separate valet key that can only open the door and start the car, preventing entry into the glove box or trunk.

- Keyless entry systems are available on many modern cars, opening door locks or a trunk lid at the press of a button. Some also activate or deactivate a car alarm system.

- Hood locks make it more difficult to open a car's hood without special keys.

- Passkey systems don't allow the car to be started without the correct electrical signal from the passkey. Some passkeys also require a password to operate.

Tow Your Car Safely

Road emergencies sometimes can be solved by following the steps given earlier in this chapter. If not, your car may need to be moved to a shop or your home garage for further work. The following sections show you how to make sure you car gets towed without becoming further damaged.

Towing Basics

Older cars were towed by simply attaching a chain between the two vehicles and driving away carefully, even though it was illegal and dangerous. Modern cars can be damaged by improper towing.

Many car manufacturers recommend that their vehicles *not* be towed using a front-end-lifting sling-type tow truck **(a)**. Check your car's owner's manual before allowing you car to be towed by a service. Most tow truck drivers are experienced and safe, but a bad decision can be costly and possibly dangerous.

Front-engine cars typically are towed using a flat-bed trailer, also known as a rollback **(b)**. The bed tilts to accept the front of the car, and chains are attached to a hoist that pulls the car up the ramp. Towing hooks are built into the front of most modern cars as attachment points.

Some car manufacturers recommend that the car be towed from the rear to minimize possible damage to the drive train.

If your car must be towed, make sure that the transmission is in a neutral gear so that the wheels can turn freely. Some cars require that the universal joint (between the transmission and differential) be disconnected and the drive line supported. Refer to the owner's manual for specific recommendations on towing your car.

Note: *If you have Emergency Road Service coverage, contact your insurance provider for assistance.*

Don't attempt to tow a car with a rope, except to pull it off the road. Also, be careful of predatory towing services. If your car is broken down on a busy thoroughfare, you may be approached by a tow truck that pulls up to offer assistance. In many cases, these trucks are independent and often *unlicensed* tow services. Some are brash enough to start connecting up your car without authorization. Your car may be towed to their lot, where you must pay exorbitant charges to get your car back. Or your car may be unsafely towed or damaged and you may not have recourse.

Instead, use a service dispatched or recommended by police or your insurance company. If you, your insurance company, or the police didn't call the tow service, don't use the service. If you have a problem with an unauthorized tow service, call the police. Once an authorized tow service arrives, read the tow invoice before signing, and ask questions as needed *before* allowing the tow service to begin hooking up to your car. If there is a law enforcement officer present, ask for assistance.

TIP

Caution

Towing your vehicle with another passenger vehicle is not recommended. Use a reputable towing service with the experience and equipment to not damage your car.

Glossary of Automotive Terms

Cars have a language of their own—from *advance* to *zerk fitting*. Following are some of the more common automotive terms and their concise definitions.

Advance   Setting the ignition timing so that a spark occurs earlier in the engine's cycle for more efficient operation.

Air bag   A restraint system that inflates a hidden bag (or bags) when a sensor at the front of the car is hit in a collision.

Air cleaner   A metal or plastic housing on or near the carburetor or fuel injection intake with a filter to remove larger particles from the air.

Air filter   A replaceable part that helps keep road dust and bugs out of the engine.

Alignment   An adjustment to keep parts in their correct relative positions, such as the alignment of a car's wheels.

Alternator   A component that converts mechanical energy into alternating current (AC) that then must be changed (rectified) into direct current (DC) for use by the car's electrical system. Also known as an AC generator.

Ammeter   An instrument that measures and reports the flow of electric current.

Antifreeze   A liquid added to water and used to keep a car's engine cool when running; the antifreeze ingredient keeps coolant from freezing in cold weather. See also *coolant*.

Antilock brake system (ABS)   An electronic system that controls hydraulics to evenly distribute a car's braking power to avoid skidding.

Automatic choke   A device that reduces air flow into a carburetor when the engine is cold, to increase the richness of the fuel/air mixture and help the engine start faster.

Automatic transmission   A device that automatically selects gears based on the car's weight and speed.

Ball joint   A ball and socket used as a joint in the steering arms.

Battery A device that produces and stores direct current (DC) by converting chemical energy into electrical energy.

Bearing A metal part that is designed to reduce friction between surfaces.

Bell housing A metal shroud that covers the engine's flywheel and the transmission's clutch or torque converter mechanisms. The starter motor often is attached to the bell housing.

Belted radial tire A tire in which the plies run radially, with two or more belts added for strength.

Bias-belted tire A bias tire with two or more belts for added strength.

Bias tire A tire with cords or layers set at an angle; found on older cars.

Body filler A hardening plastic material used to fill small dents and creases in an auto body.

Body panels Thin metal or plastic components that decoratively cover unibody cars. Their finish is relatively thin and can easily be scratched.

Bore The width of an engine's cylinder.

Brake A device that converts kinetic energy into heat energy, slowing down the car.

Brake caliper The part on a disc brake system that squeezes the disc to make the car slow or stop.

Brake drum The part on a drum brake system that receives pressure from the brake shoe.

Brake pads The replaceable surface of a disc brake system's calipers.

Brake shoe The movable part of a drum brake system that applies pressure against the brake drum; the replaceable surface of a drum brake system is the friction lining on the shoe.

Breaker-point ignition An ignition system using two contact points that are moved to interrupt the electrical current within a breaker-point or mechanical distributor; common in older cars.

BTDC (before top dead center) Any point during the upward movement of an engine piston between the bottom and top.

Bushings The rubber connections at the top and bottom of shock absorbers and struts.

Camber The inward or outward tilt of a car's wheel.

Camshaft The rotating shaft inside the engine that opens and closes valves using cams or rotating high spots.

Carburetor   A device that dumps a stream of fuel into passing air for distribution to the engine's cylinders for burning.

Caster   The backward or forward tilt of a car's front wheel axle or spindle.

Catalytic converter   An exhaust system component that changes pollutants into less harmful elements.

CID (cubic inch displacement)   The total volume of all combustion chambers in an engine measured in cubic inches. To translate engine size in liters into cubic inches, multiply liters by 61.027.

Clutch   A device that connects and disconnects the engine from the transmission, or an air conditioner compressor pulley from the compressor shaft.

Combustion chamber   The area within an engine cylinder where combustion of a fuel/air mixture takes place.

Compression ratio   The ratio of the area when a piston is at the top of its travel to that when it is at the bottom.

Connecting rod   The rod that connects an engine's crankshaft to a piston.

Constant velocity (CV) joint   A joint in a car's driveline that enables the shaft to pivot without vibration.

Coolant   A mixture of water and antifreeze that helps absorb the heat from the engine.

Cooling fan   A fan mounted on the engine side of the radiator to draw air over the radiator's finned tubes.

Cooling system   The system that removes heat from the engine.

Crankcase   The lowest part of an engine, surrounding the crankshaft.

Crankshaft   The main rotating part of an engine that turns the piston's up-and-down motion into a circular motion that can be used by the transmission and, eventually, the wheels.

Cylinder block   The largest part of the engine, including cylinders, oil passages, water jackets, and some other components.

Cylinder head   The detachable part of the engine above the cylinders, sometimes including the valves or other components.

Differential   The part of a rear-wheel-drive system that uses gears to transfer the driveline's power to two wheels as needed.

Disc brakes   A brake system that applies caliper pressure against a disc on wheels to stop the car. Typically used in the front wheels of many cars.

Distributor   A device that sends the coil's electricity evenly and at precisely the right time to the engine's spark plugs.

Double-overhead cam (DOHC)   An engine that uses two camshafts to control valves—one for the intake valves and one for the exhaust valves.

Drain cock   The small plug at the bottom of the radiator that allows coolant to be drained.

Drive belts   The rubber and fabric belts that apply the crankshaft pulley's rotation to rotate an alternator, water pump, power steering pump, and air conditioning compressor, if so equipped. Some cars use a single belt, called a serpentine drive belt, for driving many components.

Drivetrain   All components that transmit power to a car's wheels, including the clutch or torque converter, transmission, driveshaft, joints, and the differential or driveaxle.

Drum brakes   A brake system that applies brake shoes against the inside of a brake drum to stop or slow a car. Typically used in the rear wheels of many cars.

EGR valve   Part of the EGR (exhaust gas recirculation) system that recirculates some exhaust gas into the engine's air/fuel mixture to reduce emissions.

Electrical system   The components that start your car, replenish and store electricity, and operate electrical devices.

Electrolyte   Sulfuric acid and water solution within a car battery that produces electricity.

Electronic fuel injection (EFI)   A computer-controlled system that injects fuel into engine cylinders.

Electronic ignition   An automotive ignition system that uses electronic signals to interrupt the electrical voltage within the distributor—common in cars built since 1976.

Exhaust emission control   One or more devices for reducing the engine's contaminants before they go into the atmosphere.

Exhaust gas recirculation (EGR) system   A system that recirculates exhaust gases to lower engine combustion temperatures and reduce nitrogen oxides.

Exhaust manifold   A system that collects exhaust gases from the cylinders and delivers them to the exhaust pipes.

Flathead engine An engine with the valves in the engine block so that the engine's head is flat.

Flywheel A round metal wheel at the end of the crankshaft that collects and passes the engine's power to the transmission.

Four-wheel-drive A drive system that distributes the engine's power to all four wheels.

Front-wheel-drive A drive system that distributes the engine's power to the wheels at the front of the vehicle.

Fuel Any combustible substance that is burned to provide power or heat—for example, gasoline, ethanol, methanol, diesel, natural gas, or propane.

Fuel/air mixture The combustible mixture of gasoline fuel and air, fed to an automobile engine.

Fuel filter A replaceable part that attempts to keep contaminants out of the fuel used by an engine.

Fuel injection Injects metered fuel into the intake manifold at each cylinder for burning.

Fuel pump A device that draws fuel from a tank and delivers it to the fuel system.

Fuse The weakest link in an electrical circuit, designed to fail first before an electrical overload damages other components.

Fuse panel A panel where electrical fuses are mounted for easy access.

Gap Typically, the distance a spark must jump between the center electrode and the ground electrode on a spark plug.

Gasket A thin, pliable material used as a seal between two metal surfaces.

Gasoline The most common fuel used to power automobiles; refined from petroleum.

Ground The neutral side of an automotive electrical system, typically the negative terminal, that is attached or grounded to the engine or frame.

Heater core A small radiator that releases heat from the engine into the car interior.

Horsepower A complex formula for determining the power generated by an engine.

Hydraulic A system that uses hydraulic oil to transmit or magnify power.

Hydrocarbons Any compound that has hydrogen and carbon molecules, such as in gasoline, diesel, or other petroleum products.

Idle system   The system within a carburetor that maintains an even flow of fuel when the engine is idling.

Ignition coil   An electromagnetic device in a car that converts low voltage into high voltage.

Ignition module   Controls the delivery of high-voltage electrical sparks to the spark plugs.

Ignition system   The system that supplies and distributes the spark needed for combustion within the engine.

Independent suspension   A suspension system that allows two wheels on the same axle to move independently of each other.

Intake manifold   A system that distributes air (port fuel-injected systems) or a fuel/air mixture (carbureted and throttle-body injected systems) to the appropriate cylinders.

Internal combustion   The combustion or burning of fuel in an enclosed area, such as an engine's combustion chamber.

Kickdown   A switch or linkage that moves an automatic transmission into a lower gear when the accelerator pedal is pushed down.

Leaf spring   A group of flat steel springs in a car's suspension system used to minimize up-and-down motion.

Lifter   The metal part of a valve system between the cam lobe and the push rod or rocker arm.

Liter   A measurement of volume equal to 61.027 cubic inches. To translate engine size in cubic inches to liters, multiply cubic inches by .0164.

Lubrication system   The engine passages, the oil pump and filter, and related parts that lubricate the engine to reduce wear on moving parts.

MacPherson strut   A component found on most front-wheel-drive cars that combines a suspension coil spring and shock absorber in one unit.

Manual steering   An automotive steering system that doesn't use a power booster.

Manual transmission   A transmission in which the driver manually selects the operating gear.

Master cylinder   A hydraulic cylinder that magnifies the driver's foot pressure to evenly operate the four wheel brakes.

Mixture adjusting screw   A tapered screw that regulates the fuel in a carburetor's airstream.

Motor   An electromagnetic device such as a starting motor; technically a car's power source is an engine rather than a motor.

Muffler   Part of the exhaust system that reduces the sound of automotive exhaust by passing it through baffles and chambers.

OBD-II   An automotive standard for onboard diagnostics troubleshooting codes.

Octane   A unit of measurement for a fuel's tendency to detonate or knock.

Odometer   A meter that reports miles driven since the car was built or since being reset at the beginning of a trip.

OEM (original-equipment manufacturer)   The maker of parts installed on the car when built.

Oil filter   A replaceable part that removes impurities from the engine oil.

Oil pan   The removable part of an engine below the block that serves as a reservoir for the engine's oil.

Oil pump   A device that pumps lubricating oil from the oil pan through the engine as needed, to minimize wear.

Overdrive   A transmission gear designed to reduce engine speed and increase fuel economy when the car is operating at more than 50 miles per hour; some cars use a fifth gear instead of an overdrive gear.

Overhead cam (OHC) engine   An engine with the camshaft in the cylinder head instead of the engine block.

Overhead valve (OHV) engine   An engine with valves in the cylinder head instead of the engine block.

Pad wear indicator   A device that indicates when brake pads are worn to the point of needing replacement.

Parking brake   A hand- or foot-operated brake that applies brake shoes or brake pads against the braking surface on a car's rear wheels; also called an emergency brake.

Passenger-restraint system   A system of seatbelts and interlocks designed to protect passengers from injury in an accident.

Piston   The movable floor of an engine cylinder that is connected by a rod to the crankshaft.

Piston rings   The rings that fit around the side of a piston and against the cylinder wall to seal the compression chamber in an engine block.

Pitman-arm steering   A steering system that uses a gear to transmit the driver's steering motion to a swiveling component called the pitman arm.

Points   See *Breaker-point ignition*.

Positive crankcase ventilation (PCV)   A system of pipes and passages that recirculates vapors from the oil pan for burning by the engine.

Power brake booster   A hydraulic and vacuum unit that helps the brake's master cylinder magnify the driver's foot pressure to evenly operate the four-wheel brakes.

Power steering   A hydraulic unit that magnifies the driver's motion to more easily steer the car.

Push rod   A rod that connects the valve lifter to the rocker arm.

Rack-and-pinion steering   A steering system with one gear across another, making steering more responsive than Pitman-arm steering.

Radial tire   A tire with cords or layers laid radially or across the tread.

Radiator   A car component that reduces engine temperature by transferring the heat in a liquid (coolant) to the air.

Rear-wheel-drive   A drive system that distributes the engine's power to the wheels at the rear of the vehicle.

Relay   A device that delivers electricity from the *battery* to the *starter*.

Rod bearing   A smooth metal part between the crankshaft and individual connecting rods for reducing wear.

Rotor   A brake disc on a disc brake system.

Shock absorber   A cylinder that uses hydraulic fluid to dampen a wheel's up-and-down movement caused by bumps in the road.

Single-overhead cam (SOHC)   An engine that uses one camshaft in the engine's head to control both the intake valves and exhaust valves.

Spark plug   A metal-and-ceramic part that uses high-voltage electricity to ignite the compressed fuel/air mixture in the cylinder.

Stabilizer bar   A bar linking the suspension system on two wheels (front or rear) to stabilize steering during turns.

Starter   An electric motor that engages, spins, and disengages the engine's flywheel in order to start the engine.

Steering system   A system of parts that transfers the turning movements of the steering wheel to the front wheels.

Stroke   The distance a piston moves up and down within an engine cylinder.

Strut   See *MacPherson strut*.

Suspension   A group of parts (such as springs, shock absorbers, and struts) that suspends the car's frame and body or unibody above the wheels.

Thermostat   A heat-controlled valve that regulates the flow of coolant in an engine based on a preset minimum temperature.

Tie rod   A jointed rod in the steering system that ties the steering gear to the wheels.

Timing belt   A belt that synchronizes the efforts in the cylinder block with those in the cylinder head.

Timing gears   The gears that keep the *camshaft* (valves) in time with the *crankshaft* (pistons) using a timing chain or timing belt.

Toe   The position of the front edge of both front tires relative to each other.

Torque converter   An automatic clutch on an automatic transmission.

Transaxle   A transmission and differential axle combined into one unit.

Transmission   A component that transmits the engine's power to the wheels using gears.

Universal joint   A joint in a car's drive shaft that allows the shaft to pivot.

Valve   An engine component that opens and closes to control the flow of a liquid, gas, or vacuum. The intake valve lets the fuel/air mixture into, and the exhaust valve lets combusted gases out of, an engine's cylinder.

VIN (Vehicle Identification Number)   A unique 17-digit number that identifies an individual car or truck manufactured since 1980.

Voltage regulator   A device that regulates or controls the voltage output of an alternator or generator.

Water pump   A device that circulates coolant through the engine and the radiator.

Wheel cylinder   A hydraulic cylinder at each wheel that magnifies the master cylinder's pressure to evenly operate the wheel's brake system.

Wiring diagram   A drawing depicting the electrical wiring and devices in a car; useful for trouble-shooting electrical problems.

Zerk fitting   A nipple fitting installed in some suspension and steering components to allow pressurized lubricating grease to be forced into the component. Most automotive zerk fittings have been replaced with sealed fittings.

Index

W

washer fluid, 39
washing. *See* cleaning
water pump, 52
waxing, 147
wheel alignment, 114
whining noise, 181
window, 144
windshield repair, 162–163

windshield washer reservoir, 39
windshield wipers, 46–47
wiring, 89
World Manufacturer Identifier digits, 19
wrenches, 24

Z

zerk fitting, 66

![Visual Read Less–Learn More® logo]

Teach Yourself VISUALLY™ books...

Whether you want to knit, sew, or crochet . . . strum a guitar or play the piano . . . create a scrapbook or train a dog . . . make the most of Windows Vista™ or touch up your Photoshop® CS3 skills, Teach Yourself VISUALLY books get you into action instead of bogged down in lengthy instructions. All Teach Yourself VISUALLY books are written by experts on the subject and feature:

• Hundreds of color photos that demonstrate each step and/or skill

• Step-by-step instructions that accompany each photo

• Tips and FAQs that answer common questions and suggest solutions to common problems

• Information about each skill that is clearly presented on a two- or four-page spread so you can learn by seeing and doing

• A design that makes it easy to review a particular topic

Look for Teach Yourself VISUALLY books to help you learn a variety of skills—all with the proven visual learning approach you enjoyed in this book.

Make terrific crafts

NEW! Quick Tips series

978-0-7645-9641-4

978-0-470-06715-4

978-0-470-09845-5

978-0-470-09741-0

978-0-470-10150-6

978-0-7645-9640-7

978-0-470-06817-5

978-0-470-07782-5

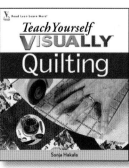

978-0-470-10149-0

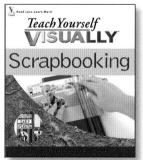

978-0-7645-9945-3

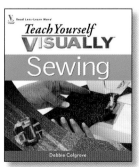

978-0-471-74991-2

designed for visual learners like you!

Make beautiful music

Make Rover behave

978-0-470-04850-4

978-0-7645-9642-1

978-0-471-74990-5

978-0-471-74989-9

Make improvements in your game

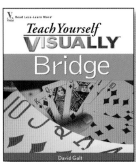

978-0-470-11424-7

978-0-470-04983-9

978-0-470-09844-8

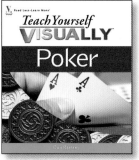

978-0-471-79906-1

Make the most of technology

978-0-470-16878-3

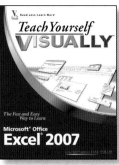

978-0-470-04595-4

978-0-470-11452-0

978-0-470-04573-2

Visual
An Imprint of WILE
Now you know.